Jack C. Richards & Chuck Sandy

Passages

Second Edition

Workbook 1

CAMBRIDGE
UNIVERSITY PRESS

CAMBRIDGE UNIVERSITY PRESS
Cambridge, New York, Melbourne, Madrid, Cape Town,
Singapore, São Paulo, Delhi, Mexico City

Cambridge University Press
32 Avenue of the Americas, New York, NY 10013-2473, USA

www.cambridge.org
Information on this title: www.cambridge.org/9780521683883

First published 1998
Second Edition 2008
16th printing 2012

Printed in Lima, Peru, by Empresa Editora El Comercio S.A.

A catalog record for this publication is available from the British Library.

ISBN 978-0-521-68386-9 student's book and self-study audio CD/CD-ROM (Windows, Mac)
ISBN 978-0-521-68388-3 workbook
ISBN 978-0-521-68387-6 teacher's edition and audio CD
ISBN 978-0-521-68390-6 CDs (audio)

Art direction, book design, and photo research: Adventure House, NYC
Layout services: TSI Graphics
Audio production: Paul Ruben Productions

Peter McDonnell: T-178

T-176 ©Adrian Judd/Archant Regional Limited
T-179 (clockwise from top left) ©Inmagine; ©Images&Stories/Alamy; ©Inmagine; ©Travelshots.com/Alamy;
T-182 ©Inmagine
T-190 ©Inmagine
T-197 (clockwise from top left) ©Inmagine; ©Brian Bailey/Getty Images; ©Inmagine; ©Jon Arnold Images Ltd./Alamy

The authors and publishers are grateful for permission to reprint the following items:
T-176 "Three Sets of Twins" by Lewis Hannam, http://www.eveningnews24.co.uk; T-180 "China Builds World's First Eco-city"
by Richard Spencer, June 7, 2006. Copyright © 2006 of Telegraph Media Group, Limited; T-184 "Cell Phone Etiquette" by
Scott Ginsberg. Scott Ginsberg is a professional speaker and the author of "HELLO my name is Scott" and "The Power of
Approachability." For more
information contact Front Porch Productions http://www.hellomynameisscott.com; T-186 "How to Cook an Egg with Your Cell
Phone" http://www.about.com; T-188 "College Students Get Podcast Lecture Options" by David Andeatta.
Reprinted with permission from the New York Post, 2006, © NYP Holdings, Inc.; T-190 "The Straight Truth About the Flexible
Drinking Straw" by Chris Broda-Bahm, Copyright © 2002 The Smithsonian's Lemelson Center; T-194 "How to Complain"

Contents

Acknowledgments

Illustration credits

Peter Hoey: 24, 39, 60, 67
Peter McDonnell: 34, 35, 52, 61
Sandy Nichols: 4, 22, 33, 64
Tyson Smith: 7, 8, 28, 45, 56, 62

Photography credits

1 ©The Garden Picture Library/Alamy. **3** ©Inmagine; ©Inmagine; ©Inmagine. **6** ©Nicola Tree/Getty Images. **10** ©Zoltan Takacs. **11** ©Melvyn Longhurst/Alamy. **13** ©Inmagine. **14** ©istockphoto. **16** ©Henry Westheim Photography/Alamy. **18** (*left to right*) ©David Young-Wolff/PhotoEdit; ©Neil Setchfield/Alamy; ©Janusz Wrobel/Alamy; ©istockphoto. **20** ©Mika/zefa/Corbis. **23** ©Rob Bartee/Alamy. **26** ©Inmagine. **27** ©Inmagine. **29** ©Inmagine. **30** ©Inmagine. **31** ©Inmagine. **36** (*top to bottom*) ©Phil Degginger/Alamy; ©Jonathan Burnett/Photo Researchers, Inc. **38** ©Mike Hill/Alamy. **40** ©Gabe Palmer/Alamy. **41** ©Inmagine. **44** (*left to right*) ©Henry Westheim Photography/Alamy; ©Christopher Bissell/Getty Images; ©Inmagine. **46** ©Don Johnston/Getty Images. **47** ©Inmagine; ©Inmagine; ©Inmagine; ©Inmagine. **48** ©Inmagine. **49** ©Inmagine. **50** ©Inmagine; ©Inmagine; ©Inmagine; ©Inmagine. **53** ©Ian Dagnall/Alamy. **54** ©Inmagine. **59** (*left to right*) ©Inmagine; ©Dennis Kitchen; ©ilian/Alamy. **63** ©Inmagine. **66** ©Michael Grecco/Getty Images. **68** ©Inmagine. **70** ©Dennis Hallinan/Alamy. **71** ©Inmagine; ©Inmagine.

Text credits

The authors and publishers are grateful for permission to reprint the following items:

6 "For Better or for Worse" by Kathleen O. Ryan, *Los Angeles Times*, Wednesday, November 1, 1995, Home Edition, Life and Style, p. 3. Copyright © 1995, Los Angeles Times. Reprinted by permission.

24 Adapted From "The Secrets of Sleep" by Michael Segell, *Esquire*, October 1994, Vol. 122, No. 4, pp. 123–127. Reprinted by permission of the author.

30 "A Ritual Loses Its Grip" by Adam Bryant, *New York Times*, Week in Review, Sunday, July 6, 1997. Copyright © 1997 by The New York Times. Reprinted by permission.

54 "The Art of Flying Solo" by Jean Seligmann. From *Newsweek*, March 1, 1993, Vol. 121, No. 9, pp. 70–73. Copyright © 1993, Newsweek, Inc. All rights reserved. Reprinted by permission.

72 "International Careers: A World of Opportunity" by Karen E. Klein, *Los Angeles Times*, Monday, September 11, 1995, Home Edition, Business, p. 17. Copyright © 1995, Los Angeles Times. Reprinted by permission.

Every effort has been made to trace the owners of copyright material in this book. We would be grateful to hear from anyone who recognizes their copyright material and who is unacknowledged. We will be pleased to make the necessary corrections in future editions of the book.

1 Friends and family

1

grammar

Which verbs and expressions can complete the sentences? Write the correct numbers of the sentences next to the verbs.

1. I _____ spending time outdoors every day.
2. I _____ to spend time outdoors every day.

a. _1_ am afraid of   g. ____ feel like
b. ____ am into   h. ____ hate
c. ____ avoid   i. ____ insist on
d. ____ can't stand   j. _1,2_ love
e. ____ don't mind   k. ____ prefer
f. ____ enjoy   l. ____ worry about

2

grammar

Read the dialogues and complete the sentences. If two answers are possible, write both of them.

1. Ada: Sam isn't happy when he has nothing to do.
    Gary: I know. It really bothers him.
    Sam can't stand _having nothing to do / to have nothing to do._

2. Vic: I hardly ever go to school parties anymore.
    Joon: Me neither. They're not as much fun as they used to be.
    Vic and Joon avoid _____

3. Tina: You visit your parents on the weekends, don't you?
    Les: Yes, I spend Sundays with them. I'm too busy the rest of the week.
    Les prefers _____

4. Tom: Are you going to take an Italian class this summer?
    Ivy: Yes, I am. I love to learn new languages.
    Ivy is into _____

5. Ang: Do you want to go rock climbing with me this weekend?
    Sue: I don't know. Rock climbing sounds dangerous!
    Sue is worried about _____

6. Josh: What sort of volunteer work do you do for the library, Celia?
    Celia: I love kids, so I volunteer as a children's storyteller on Saturdays.
    Celia enjoys _____

3
grammar

Write sentences about yourself using the verbs in the box.

am afraid of	avoid	don't mind	hate	love
am into	can't stand	enjoy	insist on	prefer

1. go shopping on the weekend

   <u>I love going shopping on the weekend.</u>

2. try different types of food

   _____

3. learn new sports or hobbies

   _____

4. meet people for my job

   _____

5. work on the weekend

   _____

6. clean and organize my room

   _____

4
vocabulary

A Match the correct words to complete the sentences.

1. Angelina volunteers at a hospital. She's very __b__.
2. Stan drives too fast and stays out late. He's _____.
3. Anna never gets angry. She's always _____.
4. Don hates a messy room. He likes being _____.
5. Tad avoids speaking out in class. He's _____.
6. Airlines hire flight attendants who enjoy meeting people and who are _____.
7. City life is crazy! In the countryside I feel more _____.
8. Lindsay insists on doing things her way. She's _____.
9. Tai never hides her true feelings. She's always _____.

a. wild and crazy
b. kind and generous
c. shy and reserved
d. friendly and outgoing
e. calm and cool
f. neat and tidy
g. honest and sincere
h. laid-back and relaxed
i. strong and independent

B Use the vocabulary above to write sentences about people you know.

1. <u>My sister is shy and reserved. She avoids meeting new people.</u>
2. _____
3. _____
4. _____
5. _____
6. _____

5
writing

A Choose the main idea for each paragraph, and write it in each blank.

> My mother loves speaking Chinese.
>
> My mother is very adventurous.
>
> I really admire my mother.
>
> I am not like my mother at all.

1. _____ . She enjoys doing unusual things and pushing herself to the limit. Last year, for example, she insisted on visiting China. She enrolled in Chinese language classes, planned her trip, and then took off across China – alone. She doesn't mind traveling alone. In fact, she enjoys going off on adventures by herself.

> I have a friend named John.
>
> My friend John and I are in the same class.
>
> My friend John is the kind of person who loves to talk.
>
> My friend John always says what is on his mind.

2. _____ . He's probably the most outspoken person I know. Last week after class, for example, he said to our teacher, "This class is really boring. Do you feel like making the class more exciting? I have some ideas." John was just saying what he thought, but our teacher didn't exactly love listening to him.

B Complete these two sentences. Then choose one of them, and write a paragraph to support it.

1. My friend _____ is the kind of person who _____

_____

2. _____ is the most _____ person I know.

_____
_____
_____
_____
_____
_____
_____
_____

grammar

Read the diary entry. Then underline the noun clauses.

Dear Diary,

I love my family — all of them, my parents and my four brothers and sisters. However, sometimes they drive me crazy. There are good and bad things about coming from a large family. One of the best things about coming from a large family is that <u>I always have someone to talk to</u>. Unfortunately, one of the disadvantages is that I never have any privacy. And of course, the trouble with not having any privacy is that I never have any space I can call my own. Our house is big, but sometimes not big enough!

grammar

Combine these two sentences into one sentence using noun clauses.

1. I'm the youngest in my family. The best thing is I'm the center of attention.
   <u>The best thing about being the youngest is that I'm the center of attention.</u>

2. I have a lot of kids. The disadvantage is I always have to clean up after them.
   _____
   _____

3. I live with my mother-in-law. The problem is we disagree about everything.
   _____
   _____

4. I have two sisters. The worst thing is they always want to know all about my personal life.
   _____
   _____

5. I have an identical twin. The trouble is no one can ever tell us apart.
   _____
   _____

3 grammar

Use noun clauses and information of your own to complete these sentences.

1. A disadvantage of having siblings who are successful is *that my parents expect me to be successful too.*

2. The problem with having a large family is _____

3. The best thing about having grandparents is _____

4. The trouble with being part of a two-income family is _____

5. One benefit of living far away from your family is _____

6. The worst thing about taking a family vacation is _____

7. An advantage of living with siblings is _____

4 vocabulary

Are the statements true or false? Check (✓) the correct answer.

	True	False
Martin's sister Sylvia married Emilio.		
1. Martin is Sylvia's great uncle.	☐	☐
2. Martin is Emilio's brother-in-law.	☐	☐
Hal's wife Nikki has a sister named Joanne.		
3. Joanne is Hal's sister-in-law.	☐	☐
4. Joanne is Hal's grandmother.	☐	☐
Hugo's daughter married Jason.		
5. Jason is Hugo's father-in-law.	☐	☐
6. Jason is Hugo's son-in-law.	☐	☐
Molly's nephew Tom has a daughter named Jennifer.		
7. Molly is Tom's aunt.	☐	☐
8. Molly is Jennifer's great-aunt.	☐	☐
Irene's father Roberto has a grandfather named Eduardo.		
9. Eduardo is Roberto's grandson.	☐	☐
10. Eduardo is Irene's great-grandfather.	☐	☐

5 reading

A Read the article. Then check (✓) your answers to the questions.

Siblings

When we are children, our siblings – that is, our brothers and sisters – are our first friends and first enemies. At the end of life, they are often our oldest friends and oldest enemies. The effect of sibling relationships in childhood can last a lifetime. Many experts say that the relationship among brothers and sisters explains a great deal about family life, especially today when brothers and sisters often spend more time with each other than with their parents.

Studies have shown that sibling relationships between sister-sister pairs and brother-brother pairs are different. Sister pairs are the closest. Brothers are the most competitive. Sisters are usually more supportive of each other. They are more talkative, frank, and better at expressing themselves and sharing their feelings. On the other hand, brothers usually have more arguments with each other.

Experts agree that relationships among siblings are influenced by many factors. For example, studies have shown that both brothers and sisters become more competitive and aggressive when their parents treat them differently from one another. However, parental treatment is not the only factor. Genetics, gender, life events, birth order, people, and experiences outside the family all shape the lives of siblings. Recently, one researcher demonstrated another factor in sibling relationships. It was discovered that children hate watching their siblings fight with each other. However, they're not afraid to take sides – supporting one sibling and punishing the other.

1. What is the main idea of the first paragraph?
   - ☐ a. Siblings are our oldest friends in life.
   - ☐ b. Some siblings have good relationships, but others have bad relationships.
   - ☐ c. Sibling relationships are among the most important relationships in life.

2. What is the main idea of the second paragraph?
   - ☐ a. Sisters get along better with their sisters than with their brothers.
   - ☐ b. Females and males generally have different sibling relationships.
   - ☐ c. Siblings spend a lot of time together because they have to.

3. What is the main idea of the third paragraph?
   - ☐ a. There are many causes of good and bad sibling relationships.
   - ☐ b. Research has shown that siblings hate to fight.
   - ☐ c. Siblings will take sides in an argument.

B Are the statements true or false? Check (✓) the correct answer. Then rewrite the false statements to make them true.

	True	False
1. Sister-brother pairs are the most competitive.	☐	☐
_____		
2. When parents treat each child a little differently, the children get along better.	☐	☐
_____		
3. Parental treatment is not the only factor that influences sibling relationships.	☐	☐
_____		
4. Children avoid watching their siblings argue.	☐	☐
_____		

vocabulary

Correct the underlined mistakes in each sentence. Write the correct form of one of the words from the box next to each sentence.

aggravate	cause	deal with	identify	ignore	run into	solve

1. Jim said I <u>solved</u> the problem with the DVD when I spilled my soda on it. ___caused___

2. Grace didn't pay her credit card bill last month. When she didn't pay it again this month, she only <u>ran into</u> her debt problem. _____

3. I always ask Kate for help with math. She can <u>ignore</u> any problem. _____

4. Tim's report was late. He <u>aggravated</u> problems with his computer that he didn't expect. _____

5. John <u>caused</u> his weight problem. He still can't fit into his old jeans! _____

6. Mike has many problems at work, so he always stays late to <u>identify</u> them. _____

7. My brother is an amazing auto mechanic. He can look at a car's engine, and <u>ignore</u> what is causing problems. _____

grammar

Circle the past modal or phrasal modal of obligation that completes each sentence.

1. I *wasn't supposed to /*(*had to*)give Mr. Lee my cell phone when he caught me texting in class.

2. Eve was worried that she *needed to / didn't have to* pass her exam to graduate.

3. Frank *didn't have to / was supposed to* take his grandmother to the store, but he wanted to.

4. I *needed to buy / shouldn't have bought* these boots, but they were on sale!

5. Bob *was supposed to / didn't need to* bring dessert to the party, but he brought an appetizer instead.

6. I *was supposed to / didn't need to* clean my apartment before my friend arrived, but I didn't have time.

3 grammar

Complete the e-mail. Use the past modals and phrasal modals of obligation in the box.

| had to | needed to | didn't have to | should have | shouldn't have | was supposed to |

New Message

Hey Ally,

I (1) __was supposed to__ pick up my brother at practice yesterday, but I forgot. Well, I didn't forget . . . I went to the mall instead. I (2) _____ go, but I wanted to see you guys. I (3) _____ thought about my brother, but I didn't. When my mom discovered that my brother (4) _____ walk home alone, she got mad at me. She said I (5) _____ forgotten about my brother. So now, I can't go to the movies tonight. My mom said it was necessary for me to think about my responsibilities, and I (6) _____ stay home as punishment.

Gigi

4 grammar

Use past modals and phrasal modals of obligation to write a sentence for each situation.

1. make a left turn
   I should have made a left turn
   instead of a right turn.

2. hand in a term paper today
   _____
   _____

3. pick up a friend from the airport
   _____
   _____

4. not eat a big lunch
   _____
   _____

5

writing

A Look at the brainstorming notes and add two more ideas to each category.

Apologizing for being late to an appointment

Do	Don't
• let the person know why you're late	• make excuses
• be sincere	• be disrespectful
• take responsibility for your lateness	• be late for a future appointment
_____	_____
_____	_____

B Complete the sentences with ideas from your brainstorming notes.

1. You need to _____ when you apologize.
2. You shouldn't _____ when you apologize.

C Choose one sentence above and brainstorm supporting ideas for the topic. Then write a paragraph based on your brainstorming notes.

> You shouldn't make excuses when you apologize. You have to simply say you are sorry. For example, if you are late for an appointment, you should never say you were confused about the meeting time. Next, you shouldn't say your directions were bad. In addition, you shouldn't blame public transportation for your lateness. . . .

_____
_____
_____
_____
_____
_____
_____
_____
_____
_____

grammar

1 Underline the modals in the sentences. Then write *C* for modals expressing degrees of certainty or *O* for modals expressing obligation, advice, or opinion.

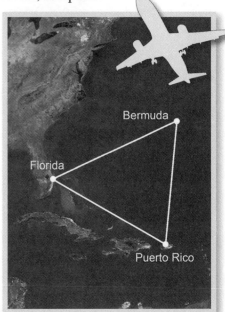

_C_ 1. Some people are certain the boats and airplanes that have disappeared in the Bermuda Triangle <u>must have</u> vanished due to human error.

_____ 2. Others believe the boats and airplanes that disappeared in the Bermuda Triangle could have been affected by supernatural forces.

_____ 3. The people who vanished should have known how to use a compass before they entered the Bermuda Triangle.

_____ 4. Experts say the people who got lost in the Bermuda Triangle must not have been prepared for strong water currents and changing weather patterns.

_____ 5. While many people have successfully navigated through the Bermuda Triangle, there are others who shouldn't have tried, as they are now missing.

grammar

2 Circle the phrase that best completes each sentence.

August 31

I just watched a documentary about the princess who died in a mysterious car accident. It was so interesting – everyone (1) *should watch* / *should have been watching* it. The princess was too young and beautiful to die in such an awful accident. Anyway, the documentary said there are many theories about how the car accident happened. Some people think the car's brakes (2) *must have been tampered* / *must have tampered* with. Others believe that the princess's driver (3) *should have caused* / *could have caused* the accident. Still others think that the princess (4) *shouldn't have gone* / *shouldn't have been going* in the car that night. Some even think the princess (5) *could have been kidnapped* / *could have kidnapped*. The police aren't even sure what really happened. I'm not sure what to believe either, but there (6) *shouldn't have been* / *must have been* a way to solve this mystery!

Comments (4)

3

grammar

Use modals expressing degrees of certainty to write your opinion about the following situations.

1. Your friend got the highest grade on a difficult English exam.

   He must have studied really hard. It's also possible the test might have been too easy.

2. You don't hear from your best friend for several days.

   _____

   _____

3. Your favorite CD is missing from your CD collection.

   _____

   _____

4. You see some very large footprints while walking in the park.

   _____

   _____

4

vocabulary

Use the verbs of belief in the box to write a sentence about each topic.

assume	be sure	figure	know for a fact
be certain	bet	guess	suppose
be positive	doubt	have a hunch	suspect

1. Elephants are the world's smartest animals.

   I am sure that elephants are the world's smartest animals.

2. The Loch Ness Monster lives in a lake in Scotland.

   _____

   _____

3. Global warming is causing a change in worldwide weather patterns.

   _____

4. People eat bananas more than any other fruit in the world.

   _____

5. Some pyramids were built over 2,000 years ago to honor Egyptian kings.

   _____

6. UFOs have visited Earth hundreds of times.

   _____

5

reading

A Read the article quickly to find the answers to the questions.

1. When did the British couple go on vacation? _____

2. Who gave the couple directions to Spain? _____

Hotel Time WARP

The idea of traveling backward or forward through time has long been a favorite subject of books, movies, and television shows. Although some scientists suspect that it may actually be possible, no one has invented a way to make it happen. However, many people have reported traveling in time.

One famous story is about a British couple who were vacationing in France in 1979. They were looking for a place to stay for the night and noticed a sign for an old circus. They found a hotel nearby and discovered that almost everything inside the hotel was made of heavy wood and there were no modern conveniences such as telephones or televisions. Furthermore, their room doors did not have locks, and the windows had wooden shutters instead of glass. In the morning, two police officers entered the hotel wearing old-fashioned uniforms with capes. After getting confusing directions from the officers to Spain, the couple paid their amazingly inexpensive hotel bill and left.

Two weeks later, the couple returned to France and decided to stay at the odd, but very cheap, hotel again. This time, however, the hotel was nowhere to be found. Positive that they were in the exact same spot because of the circus posters, the couple realized that the hotel had completely vanished. Even more confusing, they found that the photographs they had taken inside the hotel did not develop. Later, their research uncovered that the French officers had been wearing uniforms worn before the year 1905.

Scientists analyzing these events call them "time slips" and believe that they must happen randomly and spontaneously. However, up to now, scientists cannot explain why, when, or how they occur. But when they do occur, people are so bewildered and confused that they can barely explain what happened to them, even though they are sure they have experienced some sort of time travel.

B Read the article again. Check (✓) the statements you think the author would agree with.

☐ 1. Time travel is not a favorite subject of books, movies, and television shows.

☐ 2. Few people have reported traveling through time.

☐ 3. Scientists have invented a way to make time travel happen.

☐ 4. Photographs taken in old hotels do not develop.

☐ 5. Scientists cannot explain why, when, or how "time slips" occur.

☐ 6. Many people believe they have traveled through time.

3 Exploring new cities

1

grammar

Underline the relative clauses in the letter. Then add commas where necessary.

July 15

Dear Mom and Dad,

Greetings from Maine where the water is too cold for us to go swimming, but the scenery is beautiful. We're having a great time, and we've enjoyed every place that we've visited. This week we're in Bar Harbor which is a lovely island town. The place is absolutely full of tourists! Tonight we're going for a ride on a boat that will take us to one of the nearby islands. Our friend James who lives here has already taken us hiking and to the Bar Harbor Music Festival. It's been fun! That's it for now. We miss you.

Love, Sarah and Eric

2

grammar

Join the following sentences using non-defining relative clauses.

1. Many tourists enjoy seeing the Kuala Lumpur skyline in Malaysia. It includes some of the tallest skyscrapers in the world.

   <u>Many tourists enjoy seeing the Kuala Lumpur skyline in Malaysia,</u>
   <u>which includes some of the tallest skyscrapers in the world.</u>

2. People visit Washington, D.C., in the springtime. They can see the cherry blossoms in bloom in April.

   _____

   _____

3. The cherry trees in Washington, D.C., were a gift from the Japanese government to the U.S. They are admired by everyone.

   _____

   _____

4. Thousands of years ago, people in Mexico began to grow corn. Corn continues to be a very important food in Mexico today.

   _____

   _____

5. The tortilla is typically eaten in Mexico. It is a thin, flat bread.

   _____

   _____

3

vocabulary

Circle the correct words to complete the sentences.

1. When preparing to host the 2000 Olympics, Sydney updated its
   hotels / climate / (*transportation system*) with improvements to its commuter rail.

2. New York City has hundreds of restaurants offering a wide variety of
   climates / cuisines / green spaces, including Italian, Chinese, Brazilian, and Indian.

3. Many people are moving from bigger cities to smaller towns because the
   cost of living / landmarks / nightlife is more affordable.

4. If you enjoy *neighborhoods / shopping / nightlife*, you'll love the music and
   live shows in Rio de Janeiro.

5. Some people think Reykjavik, Iceland, is cold in the wintertime,
   but surprisingly, it has a very mild *climate / cuisine / transportation system*
   during the winter months.

6. Some famous *hotels / neighborhoods / landmarks* in London include
   Buckingham Palace and the Tower of London.

7. Many cities are actively preserving *green spaces / hotels / cuisines* in
   their downtown areas for people to have picnics, walk their dogs,
   and enjoy outdoor concerts.

4

grammar

Use defining or non-defining relative clauses to write sentences about these topics.

- a popular tourist activity in your city
- a town with many historical attractions
- a place with a good climate
- an excellent city for shopping

1. Tourists in New York City like to ride the Staten Island Ferry, which is free and has wonderful views of New York Harbor.

2. _____

3. _____

4. _____

5 *writing*

A Look at the phrases in the box about Chiang Mai. Choose the main idea and write it in the center of the mind map. The write the supporting details in the mind map.

reasonable prices
fruits and spices
a wonderful night market

clothing
handicrafts
jewelry

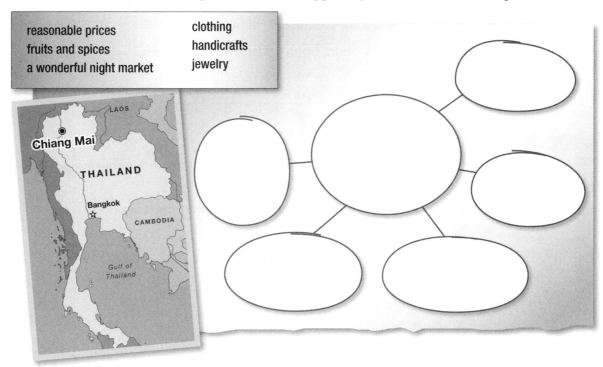

B Now read the paragraph about Chiang Mai, Thailand. Answer the questions.

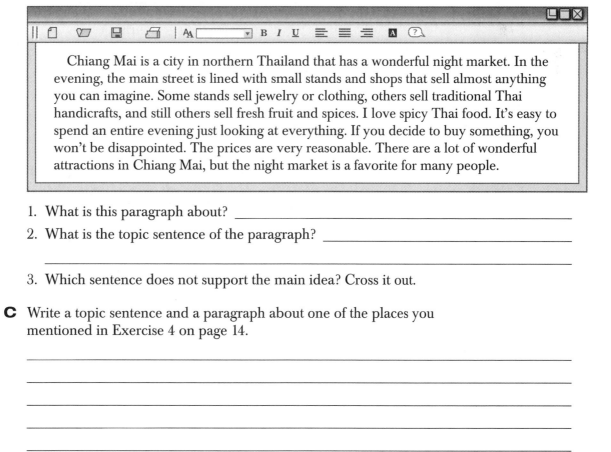

> Chiang Mai is a city in northern Thailand that has a wonderful night market. In the evening, the main street is lined with small stands and shops that sell almost anything you can imagine. Some stands sell jewelry or clothing, others sell traditional Thai handicrafts, and still others sell fresh fruit and spices. I love spicy Thai food. It's easy to spend an entire evening just looking at everything. If you decide to buy something, you won't be disappointed. The prices are very reasonable. There are a lot of wonderful attractions in Chiang Mai, but the night market is a favorite for many people.

1. What is this paragraph about? _____

2. What is the topic sentence of the paragraph? _____
   _____

3. Which sentence does not support the main idea? Cross it out.

C Write a topic sentence and a paragraph about one of the places you mentioned in Exercise 4 on page 14.

_____
_____
_____
_____
_____
_____

LESSON B · My kind of town

grammar

1 Complete the sentences by unscrambling the phrases given.

1. a / dynamic / port / with a 24-hour shopping mall / city
   Singapore is <u>a dynamic port city with a</u>
   <u>24-hour shopping mall.</u>

2. a / European / city / quaint / old / with a lovely castle
   Prague is _____
   _____

3. a / trading center / with huge skyscrapers / modern /
   Taipei is _____
   _____

4. a / with fascinating old buildings / charming / city
   Salvador is _____
   _____

5. a / industrial / modern / large / city / with a beautiful lakeshore
   Chicago is _____

6. an / with world-famous theme parks / exciting / tourist destination
   Orlando is _____

vocabulary

2 Use the words in the box to complete the sentences.

border	coastal	college	mountain	port	rural	tourist

1. Ana lives in a ____<u>rural</u>____ town. The nearest city is over two hours away.

2. The local university employs most of the people living in this _____ town.

3. _____ towns are usually near the ocean or a river where ships unload cargo.

4. People travel from the U.S. to Mexico through the _____ town of Calexico.

5. I work in a small _____ town with great beaches and seafood places.

6. We stopped in a crowded _____ town full of overpriced souvenir shops.

7. Nick lives in a _____ town that is nearly 3,000 meters above sea level.

3

grammar

Use the words in parentheses to combine the sentences.

1. The streets are well lit, but it's best to be careful at night.   (in spite of)
   <u>In spite of the well-lit streets, it's best to be careful at night.</u>

2. There is a crime problem, but it's still a wonderful place to visit.   (despite)
   _____

3. The shopping malls are crowded, but people aren't buying much.   (although)
   _____

4. It snows a lot, but I still like living here.   (even though)
   _____

5. My city is on the ocean, but the water there is too polluted for people
   to go swimming. (however)
   _____

6. The city center is very picturesque, but there's not much to do.   (nevertheless)
   _____

7. There's a lot to do here at night, but it's a very noisy neighborhood.
   (on the other hand)
   _____

4

grammar

Complete the sentences with your own opinions about cities you know.

1. In spite of ____the pollution____ , ____Los Angeles____ would be an ideal place to live.

2. The worst thing about _____ is _____ .
   Nevertheless, _____ .

3. The best thing about _____ is _____ .
   However, _____ .

4. Even though _____ has a lot of _____ ,
   _____ .

5. The weather in _____ is _____ .
   On the other hand, _____ .

6. _____ would be a great place to live. However, _____
   _____ .

7. Although _____ is a favorite tourist destination for many, it also has
   its problems. For example, _____ .

5 reading

A Match the words in the box with the photos. Then read two articles about megacities.

| auto emissions | carpooling | a landfill | public transportation |

1. _carpooling_   2. _____   3. _____   4. _____

MEGACITIES: TWO VIEWS

1 The world's population is not only growing, it is also becoming more urbanized. An increasing number of people are moving to cities in the hope of having a better life. The cities promise steady work and higher salaries. With more money, people think they can provide for their families more easily.

As the population becomes more urbanized, megacities are created. Yes, there are more jobs in urban areas, but is the quality of life better in these megacities? A quick survey of several major cities reveals some of their problems: Pollution from auto emissions is poisoning the air; landfills are overflowing with garbage. With declining resources and growing competition, sometimes there is not enough food. These are all very serious problems.

We cannot get rid of megacities – they are here to stay. What we should concentrate on, however, is building "villages" inside the cities. These "urban villages" could be self-sufficient and grow their own food. The members of these villages would recycle and do very little damage to the environment. The villages would serve the needs of the local people, not big business. We need to limit large-scale development, not encourage it.

> **megacity**
> a city with a population of ten million or more

2 It's true that megacities have problems, but these have been exaggerated. The truth of the matter is that people move to cities to escape their hard life in the country. Urban areas, even with their problems, offer people a better life than in rural areas. The old ways of life in rural areas have broken down, and it is now very difficult to make a living as a farmer.

People live longer in the cities. Medical care is better there. And, of course, employment opportunities can be found everywhere in the city. We should continue to develop city services so that people can enjoy their lives in the world's urban centers.

Rather than limiting development, we should encourage it. Public transportation systems need to be developed so that people can travel to and from work and school easily. Carpooling should be encouraged to cut down on pollution. The more we clean up and develop our megacities, the more life will improve for the residents of those cities.

B Match the statements with the articles that would support them.

	1	2	1 & 2
1. "Megacities have problems."	☐	☐	☐
2. "Life in rural areas is hard."	☐	☐	☐
3. "We should recreate village life in the cities."	☐	☐	☐
4. "There are more chances to work in the cities."	☐	☐	☐
5. "Continued development will hurt the quality of life."	☐	☐	☐
6. "Continued development can improve the quality of life."	☐	☐	☐

LESSON A · It's about time!

1

grammar

Combine the sentences using the words in parentheses. Use reduced clauses wherever possible.

1. Classes are over for the day. I often go out with my friends.   (after)

   <u>After classes are over for the day, I often go out with my friends.</u>

2. I lost my watch. I've been late for all my appointments.   (ever since)

   _____

3. You should relax and count to ten. You start to feel stressed.   (as soon as)

   _____

4. I go for a run. I stretch for at least fifteen minutes.   (right before)

   _____

5. You shouldn't listen to music. You are studying for a big test.   (while)

   _____

6. I watch TV. I fall asleep.   (until)

   _____

2

grammar

Read the statements. Are they true for you? Check (✓) true or false. Then rewrite the false statements to make them true.

	True	False
1. Whenever I get stressed out, I take a walk and try to relax.	☐	✓

   <u>I usually munch on snacks whenever I get stressed out.</u>
   <u>I like crunchy snacks like pretzels and popcorn.</u>

	True	False
2. As soon as I get to work, I check my e-mail and phone messages.	☐	☐
3. Ever since I started studying English, I've had more homework.	☐	☐
4. I like to read the newspaper while I'm eating lunch.	☐	☐
5. After I fall asleep, nothing can wake me up.	☐	☐

3

vocabulary

Use the phrases from the box to complete the conversations.

| burn out |
| calm down |
| chill out |
| drop off |
| perk up |
| turn in |

1. A: I lost my car keys! I'm going to be late for my doctor's appointment!
   B: You need to _____calm down_____. Relax. Maybe you can reschedule.

2. A: You look tired. You need to _____ before our meeting.
   B: Yeah, you're right. Maybe I should have a cup of coffee.

3. A: Poor Jenny. She has two papers to write and a final exam to study for.
   B: That's a lot of work. I hope she doesn't _____ before graduation.

4. A: My flight leaves tomorrow morning at six o'clock.
   B: You should _____ early tonight so you'll wake up on time.

5. A: What a day! I had three meetings and a business lunch. I'm so tired.
   B: Let's have some dinner. Then let's _____ and watch TV.

6. A: I've been having a lot of trouble falling asleep lately.
   B: Try drinking warm milk. It usually helps me _____ quickly.

4

grammar

Use time clauses to complete the sentences so they are true for you.

1. _As soon as_____ I get home from work, I _change into some comfortable_____
   _clothes and make a big bowl of popcorn._____

2. _____ I have the chance to chill out, _____
   _____

3. _____ I met my best friend, we _____
   _____

4. _____ I started riding a bike, I _____
   _____

5. _____ eating a large meal, I _____
   _____

5

writing

A Read the paragraph and choose the best topic sentence. Is each topic sentence too general, too specific, or just right? Check (✓) the correct answer.

1. _____

We experience a gradual rise of energy in the morning, peaking around noon. There is a slow decline in energy in the midafternoon with a second peak early in the evening. This is followed by a steady decline in energy until bedtime. Everyone experiences these energy patterns. They are a part of daily life.

	Too general	Too specific	Just right
a. People need energy to get through the day.	☐	☐	☐
b. People's energy patterns change according to the time of day.	☐	☐	☐
c. Everyone's energy peaks around noon.	☐	☐	☐

2. _____

Newborn babies sleep an average of 18 hours a day, but as children grow older, they sleep less. However, when children reach their teens, they seem to need a lot of sleep again. It is not unusual for teenagers to sleep until noon on weekends, if their parents let them. When people reach old age, they tend to sleep much less than they did in their forties and fifties.

	Too general	Too specific	Just right
a. People's sleep needs change as they go through life.	☐	☐	☐
b. Babies sleep more than elderly people.	☐	☐	☐
c. Everyone needs sleep.	☐	☐	☐

3. _____

In fact, Americans now spend over $1 billion a year on vitamins and food supplements. Vitamin companies know this and supply an almost endless variety of vitamins. There are multivitamins for adults, special vitamins for women, flavored vitamins for children, and even vitamins to help students study better. New types of vitamin pills come out almost monthly, and there is at least one vitamin store in every shopping mall.

	Too general	Too specific	Just right
a. Vitamins supplement a healthy diet.	☐	☐	☐
b. Vitamin pills are popular with women.	☐	☐	☐
c. In the U.S., vitamins are big business.	☐	☐	☐

B Write a topic sentence about tips for staying healthy or how and when you should exercise. Then write a paragraph that supports your main idea.

_____

_____

1
vocabulary

Rewrite the sentences by replacing the underlined words with the phrases in the box. Sometimes more than one answer is possible.

drift off
fast asleep
feel drowsy
have a sleepless night
nod off
sleep like a log
sound asleep
take a power nap
toss and turn
wide awake

1. If Elisa is worried when she goes to bed, she is <u>unable to sleep</u>.

   If Elisa is worried when she goes to bed, she tosses and turns.

   If Elisa is worried when she goes to bed, she has a sleepless night.

2. My father always <u>falls asleep</u> after eating a heavy meal.

   _____

3. Simon often <u>sleeps for a few minutes</u> to boost his creativity at work.

   _____

4. As soon as Sue's head hits the pillow, she falls <u>into a deep sleep</u>.

   _____

5. San-chien is lucky he <u>sleeps heavily</u> because his roommate snores so loudly!

   _____

6. Liz isn't tired at all. In fact, she's <u>completely alert</u>!

   _____

7. Marina often <u>begins to feel sleepy</u> when she reads on the train or in a car.

   _____

2
grammar

Circle the word or phrase that best completes each sentence.

1. *Considering that / Just in case /* (*Unless*) I'm really worried, I usually sleep well.

2. *Even if / Just in case / Only if* I have bad dreams, I don't recall the details later.

3. *Even if / As long as / Unless* I sleep well, I wake up feeling rested.

4. *Considering that / Only if / Unless* I didn't sleep last night, I feel pretty good.

5. Bring an umbrella with you *only if / as long as / just in case* it rains later.

3

grammar

Use the information in the box and the expressions in parentheses to write sentences.

I'm completely exhausted.
I sleep deeply.
I drink too much caffeine during the day.
I forget to set my alarm clock.
I've slept well the night before.
I get thirsty in the middle of the night.

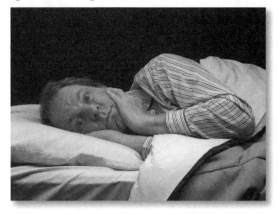

1. Sometimes I have trouble drifting off.   (even if)

   Sometimes I have trouble drifting off, even if I'm completely exhausted.

2. I always feel great in the morning.   (as long as)

   _____

3. My neighbors listen to loud music every night.   (considering that)

   _____

4. I never oversleep in the morning.   (unless)

   _____

5. I keep a glass of water by my bed.   (just in case)

   _____

6. I have trouble falling asleep.   (only . . . if)

   _____

4

grammar

Answer these questions using clauses with *considering that, as long as, even if, unless, (just) in case,* or *only . . . if.*

1. Do you stay awake thinking, or do you fall asleep as soon as you lie down?

   I only stay awake thinking if I'm having a problem at work.

2. Are you usually alert or still sleepy when you first get up in the morning?

   _____

3. Do you ever take naps during the day, or do you wait until bedtime to sleep?

   _____

4. Do you sleep like a log all night, or do you toss and turn?

   _____

5. Do you always need eight hours of sleep a night, or can you survive on less?

   _____

A Read the article quickly to find the answers to these questions.

reading

1. What causes snoring? _____

2. What is sleep apnea? _____

_____

The Problem with SNORiNG

If you don't snore now, you probably will. The majority of men and women over 40 snore. In most cases, weight gain is the cause of chronic snoring. However, a third of the people who start snoring in middle age have no problem with their weight. As we get older, the muscles in our throat lose their tone so that they vibrate as air passes over them. The result is snoring.

Snoring can cause serious problems in a relationship, but even more importantly, snoring is associated with some serious medical problems. People who snore are at greater risk for high blood pressure and heart disease. Moreover, snoring can lead to a condition called sleep apnea. A person with sleep apnea actually stops breathing for several seconds and then wakes up breathless. This can happen hundreds of times a night, but often the person has no memory of these episodes in the morning. The condition is dangerous. Every year, 38,000 people die of sleep apnea because they do not wake up in time. People with serious

sleep apnea do not get much sleep, and during the day they feel very tired. This is usually what leads them to seek medical help. If you're a snorer who is very sleepy during the day but believe you sleep well at night, you may have sleep apnea and should get medical advice.

If your only problem is snoring, though, here are a few things that might help:

• Sleep on your stomach or side instead of your back. Most snoring occurs when you sleep on your back. If necessary, sew a tennis ball to the back of your pajamas. This will wake you up when you roll onto your back.

• If you need some help getting to sleep, try taking a bath before bed.

• Lose some weight. Excess weight is the leading cause of snoring.

• If you don't have insomnia, drink coffee or soft drinks that contain caffeine an hour or two before going to bed. Snoring is the strongest during deep sleep. Caffeine in your body will make your sleep lighter and your snoring less intense.

B Read the article again. What should these people do and why?

1. Kristina thinks she sleeps well, but she feels tired and sleepy all day.

   Kristina should seek medical help because she may suffer from
   sleep apnea.

2. Kate sleeps on her back and snores loudly through the night.

   _____

   _____

3. Rick is very overweight. He keeps his wife awake with his snoring every night.

   _____

   _____

4. Angela sleeps deeply and then starts snoring loudly.

   _____

   _____

5 Communication

LESSON A · Making conversation

1

grammar

Are these customs similar to or different from customs in your culture? Check (✓) your answer. For the customs that are different, write an explanation.

	Similar	Different
1. It's customary in Japan to take your shoes off when entering a home.	☐	☐

In my culture, _____

_____

| 2. In Greece, it's not unusual to kiss friends and relatives on both cheeks when meeting them. | ☐ | ☐ |

_____

_____

| 3. In some countries, owning a pet like a dog, a cat, or a bird is considered inappropriate. | ☐ | ☐ |

_____

_____

| 4. In the U.S., arriving 30 minutes early to a dinner party isn't a good idea. | ☐ | ☐ |

_____

_____

2

vocabulary

Circle the word or phrase that best describes how each situation is viewed in your culture. Then write a sentence explaining your opinion.

1. saying hello to strangers ((normal)/ inappropriate / appropriate)
   Saying hello to strangers in my culture is considered normal.

2. opening a door for someone   (bad form / strange / polite)

_____

3. splitting a restaurant bill with a friend   (an insult / a compliment / typical)

_____

4. offering your seat on a bus to a schoolchild   (unusual / offensive / normal)

_____

5. chewing food with your mouth open   (rude / polite / typical)

_____

3
grammar

Use the information in the chart to make sentences about the dos and don'ts of customs in the U.S. Use the infinitive form of the verb in your answers.

Customs in the U.S.	
Dos	**Don'ts**
Acceptable: Use hand gestures while speaking.	Inappropriate: Talk about religion or politics.
Not unusual: Ask people how they feel.	Not a good idea: Ask about someone's salary.
Customary: Ask what someone does for a living.	Rude: Tell someone he or she has gained weight.

1. <u>It's acceptable to use hand gestures while speaking.</u>

2. _____

3. _____

4. _____

5. _____

6. _____

4
grammar

Use gerunds to rewrite the sentences you wrote above.

1. <u>Gesturing with your hands while speaking is acceptable.</u>

2. _____

3. _____

4. _____

5. _____

6. _____

5
grammar

What should people know about your customs? Write sentences with infinitive phrases or gerunds.

1. meeting business associates

<u>When you meet business associates in my culture, it's typical to exchange business cards. / When you meet business associates in my culture, exchanging business cards is typical.</u>

2. getting married

_____

_____

_____

_____

3. eating out _____

_____

_____

writing

A Read the letters seeking advice from Maggie, a newspaper columnist. Check (✓) how each writer feels about the news about Bobby. More than one answer is possible.

	Proud	Jealous	Shocked	Worried	Angry
Bad Brother					
Bobby's Pal					
Doubtful Dad					

Dear **Maggie,**

Dear Maggie,

My younger brother just told us that he's been accepted to his first-choice university. He'll be the first person in our family to go to college. I went into the family business instead of going to college. Sometimes I wonder if I made the right decision.

Bobby always gets what he wants. I can't be happy for him when I'm so envious of his success. How can I get over my feelings?

—*Bad Brother*

Dear Maggie,

I just heard that my friend Bobby has decided to attend a well-known university in the fall. Bobby and I are high school seniors, and we've talked about traveling around Europe together after high school. I'm mad that he made this decision without even telling me!

I need to talk to Bobby about this, but I'm not sure what to say. Please help!

—*Bobby's Pal*

Dear Maggie,

My son just announced that he is going away to school. Bobby is a good student, and I am very proud of him. Any college would be lucky to have him. My concern is that he's never lived away from home before. Will he be able to take care of himself? What if there's an emergency?

Give me some advice so that I can relax!

—*Doubtful Dad*

B Imagine you are Maggie. Write a response to one of the letters. Include your reaction to the problem, and offer some advice.

Dear _____ ,

_____

_____

_____

_____

_____

grammar

Read Victoria and Alicia's conversation about movie stars and the sentences below. One mistake is underlined in each sentence. Rewrite the sentences with correct verb tenses.

Victoria: Did you see the new *Star Week*? Jenny Alison broke up with Bud Pipp!

Alicia: When did they break up?

Victoria: It happened last week.

Alicia: Poor Jenny. Is she upset?

Victoria: Actually, she's not. That's what it says here in *Star Week*.

Alicia: Really? Let me see that.

Victoria: Yeah. She is dating Kevin Casey now!

1. Victoria told Alicia that Jenny Alison <u>did break up</u> with Bud Pipp.

   Victoria told Alicia that Jenny Alison had broken up with Bud Pipp.

2. Alicia asked Victoria when they <u>were breaking up</u>.

   _____

3. Victoria told Alicia that it <u>was happening</u> last week.

   _____

4. Alicia asked Victoria if Jenny <u>is</u> upset.

   _____

5. Victoria told Alicia that Jenny <u>will not be</u> upset at all.

   _____

6. Victoria <u>asked</u> Alicia that Jenny is dating Kevin Casey now.

   _____

grammar

Read the conversation. Use reported speech to complete the sentences.

Mark: Sandra, sit down. Did you hear about Paul Alvaro?

Sandra: No, I didn't. What happened?

Mark: He got a promotion.

Sandra: When did it happen?

Mark: Yesterday. The official announcement will be made soon.

1. Mark told Sandra _to sit down._ _____
2. He asked her _____
3. She said that _____
4. She asked Mark _____
5. Mark said that Paul _____
6. Sandra asked Mark _____
7. Mark said that it _____
8. He said that the official announcement _____

vocabulary

Complete this blog entry with expressions from the box. Sometimes more than one answer is possible.

she claimed that	she explained that	she told us that
she encouraged me to	she told me to	she wanted to know

---

http://www.cup.org/blogspot/   Q- Search

News ▼

NOVEMBER 10

My technology teacher gave us a horrible assignment today. (1) __She told us that__ we have to prepare a ten-minute oral presentation for Friday. I can't stand speaking in front of class. Anyway, I asked my teacher if I could do a different assignment – like a written report. (2) _____ why I didn't want to do the presentation, so I told her how nervous I get when I have to speak. (3) _____ she couldn't change the assignment for me. But she did have some advice. (4) _____ get to work on the assignment right away. Then (5) _____ practice my presentation with a friend. (6) _____ if I practiced my presentation ahead of time, I would feel more comfortable on the day I actually had to give it. So, I hope Rita can come over tomorrow and listen to my presentation. Are you reading this, Rita? Please say yes!

💬 COMMENTS (12)   ✉ E-MAIL THIS

---

reading

A Read the article. Find the boldfaced words that match the definitions.

1. strong connection _____bond_____

2. hidden _____

3. made something less important _____

4. eliminate _____

5. a feeling of closeness _____

6. finalize _____

A Ritual Loses Its GRIP

By most accounts, handshakes started as a way to show that neither person was holding a weapon. Desmond Morris, the anthropologist, calls the handshake a "tie-sign" because of the **bond** it creates. Through the centuries, the growing use of the handshake reflected greater equality among individuals, and it was used to **seal** agreements. The handshake became a friendly greeting, a sign of respect, a bet that new faces would be remembered.

Handshakes can be bad for your health. The Massachusetts Medical Society recently started an advertising campaign that encourages people to wash their hands more often, pointing out in one radio spot that "any friendly handshake can carry many illnesses."

Robert E. Swindle, a retired business professor in Peoria, Arizona, wants to **abolish** handshaking altogether. After all, now that most people don't carry **concealed** weapons in their hands, the ritual has lost its usefulness, he said.

But if Mr. Swindle got his way, something would clearly be lost in society. Allen Konopacki, who runs a sales training company in Chicago, tried an experiment last year to better understand the handshake effect. "A handshake," Mr. Konopacki said, "creates a higher level of trust, a degree of **intimacy**, within a matter of seconds."

Some sociologists say the apparent drop in the traditional value of a handshake reflects a general decline of loyalty in American society to institutions like marriage and between employers and their workers.

But Alan Wolfe, a sociologist at Boston University, disagreed. He said that while the handshake has been **devalued** by those in the media spotlight, the gesture carries just as much weight as it always has among most people because so many face-to-face encounters have been replaced by phones, faxes, and e-mail. "The handshake is really reserved for special moments," he said.

And you never know when such moments might arise. In January, a small group of men were moved to shake the hands of staff members in a bank in central Italy. It was, after all, a special time for everyone involved. The men were about to leave, having just finished robbing the bank.

B Match each person or group to the statements they would agree with.

1. Desmond Morris __d__
2. Massachusetts Medical Society _____
3. Robert E. Swindle _____
4. Allen Konopacki _____
5. Some sociologists _____
6. Alan Wolfe _____

a. Shaking hands is an unnecessary ritual.

b. The ritual of handshaking is just as important as it used to be.

c. People shake hands less often because they are not as loyal to one another.

d. Shaking hands brings people together.

e. There is a positive outcome when you shake hands.

f. Shaking hands can be unhealthy.

Check (✓) the sentences that have grammatical mistakes. Then rewrite them using the correct verb tenses.

grammar

1. ☑ A government spokesperson has announced new economic policies yesterday.

   <u>A government spokesperson announced new economic policies yesterday.</u>

2. ☐ Unusual weather events have been happening across the country.

   _____

3. ☐ Police arrested several identity thieves so far this year.

   _____

4. ☐ Burglars have stolen two paintings on Monday night.

   _____

5. ☐ Several observers saw a rare butterfly in Central Park over the past week.

   _____

6. ☐ Jazz pianist Jacqueline Gray gave a concert at the Civic Center last night.

   _____

7. ☐ The stock market has fallen sharply the other day.

   _____

Circle the verbs that best complete the news story.

grammar

The County Municipal Airport (1) (*has delayed*) / *has been delaying* a flight to London. The delay (2) *has occurred* / *has been occurring* because airline personnel (3) *have been trying* / *tried* to locate a snake inside the plane. While information is incomplete at this time, we do know a few things. As flight attendants were preparing for takeoff, several passengers saw a snake under their seats. The pilot alerted the flight control tower, and the flight was delayed in order to find the snake. Crewmembers (4) *have searched* / *have been searching* the plane ever since. They still (5) *haven't been locating* / *haven't located* the snake. They think it (6) *has hidden* / *hid* under the floor of the first-class cabin. Technicians (7) *have removed* / *have been removing* a section of the cabin floor. All the passengers (8) *have left* / *have been leaving* the plane already. They (9) *have sat* / *have been sitting* inside the terminal enjoying free soft drinks and snacks.

vocabulary

Match these headlines with the news events in the box.

| epidemic | hijacking | natural disaster | political crisis | robbery | scandal |

Millions Found in President's Secret Bank Account

Airline Passengers Still Being Held Captive

1. ____scandal____   2. _____   3. _____

Prime Minister Resigns!

4. _____   5. _____   6. _____

grammar

Complete these sentences about the headlines above. Note the use of the present perfect and the present perfect continuous.

1. Country officials say _the president's wife has been withdrawing hundreds of_ _thousands of dollars from the national account for the past three years._ _The president has denied stealing any money._

2. A bank robber has stolen _____
   _____

   The bank robber has been hiding _____
   _____

3. Passengers on Flight 200 have been _____
   _____

   The hijackers have demanded _____
   _____

4. The earthquake has destroyed _____
   _____

   Many people have been donating _____
   _____

writing

A Read the news story below. Then number the pictures in the order in which they happened.

a

b

c

d

Trapped Cat Looks Back

After spending 14 days trapped inside the walls of a 157-year-old building in New York City last April, Molly briefly became a world-famous cat. Attempting to save the black cat, rescuers set traps and used special cameras and a raw fish to try to lure Molly out from between the walls. They even tried using kittens to appeal to the cat's motherly side so she would come out, but Molly would not budge. Finally, after they removed bricks and drilled holes into the walls, someone was able to pull the curious cat out of the tiny space.

The bricks have now been replaced, but Molly has been getting visits from tourists daily since she was rescued. Even so, Molly's adventures may not be over. Her owners say that at least once they have caught her looking inside the same hole.

B Read the news story again. Underline the present perfect and present perfect continuous verbs.

C Write an article about some interesting recent news. Use the present perfect, present perfect continuous, and simple past.

_____
_____
_____
_____
_____
_____
_____

Circle the correct expressions to complete the sentences.

1. I was surprised when I won the lottery. *The moment / The next day / (Until that time,)* I had never won anything.

2. I felt awful about breaking my friend's cell phone. *Afterward / When / Until that time,* I offered to replace it.

3. Despite my fear, I loved the ride. *The moment / Up until then / Later,* I had never been on an airplane.

4. On Saturday, my mother left an urgent message on my voice mail. *Until that time / Later / As soon as* I got it, I called her back.

5. I had a delicious meal on Sunday. *The next day / When / Up until then,* however, I came down with a serious case of food poisoning.

6. When I walked in the room, everyone yelled "Happy Birthday!" *As soon as / Before that / Afterward,* I'd never been given a surprise party.

7. I got a big promotion at work. *Until that time / When / Later,* while I was telling my parents, I felt really proud.

Complete the sentences. Use the past perfect or the simple past tense of the verbs given.

1. I couldn't figure out why she looked so familiar. Later, I _____realized_____ (realize) she was my sixth-grade teacher.

2. I knew it was the mail carrier knocking on my door. As soon as I _____ (open) the door, he _____ (give) me a big package.

3. While hiking, we suddenly realized we were lost and didn't have a compass. Up until then, we _____ (not be) worried.

4. I had never experienced anything so exciting. Until that time, my life _____ (be) very uneventful.

5. I went to the airport and booked the next flight. Afterward, I _____ (wait) for the announcement to board the plane.

6. It was my first time to run a marathon. When I _____ (see) the finish line in front of me, I _____ (feel) relieved.

7. It was my first driver's license. The moment I _____ (receive) it in the mail, I _____ (begin) to dance.

8. My father was moved by the performance. Before that, I _____ (never see) him cry.

vocabulary

Use expressions from the boxes to complete the conversation.

it all started when	the next thing we knew	the thing you have to know is

Andy: Hi, Sue. I heard you and Elle got lost on your way to the big game.

Sue: Yeah. (1) _It all started when_ we began singing along with this cool CD.

Andy: What happened?

Sue: Well, we were having such a good time that (2) _____ , we'd missed the turn for the stadium.

Andy: How did you do that?

Sue: (3) _____ , we were singing and not paying attention to the road signs.

meanwhile	the other thing was	I forgot to mention

Andy: Didn't you notice you'd gone past your turn?

Sue: Yes. (4) _____ , we'd driven about 40 miles too far!

Andy: 40 miles? Wow!

Sue: And (5) _____ , we ran out of gas.

Andy: You ran out of gas? On the highway?

Sue: No, not the highway. (6) _____ that we'd decided to take a shortcut.

I forgot to mention	to make a long story short

Andy: Did you make it to the game?

Sue: Yes. But it took us about three hours to get there!

Andy: Are you kidding?

Sue: (7) _____ we also stopped for pizza.

Andy: You were hungry?

Sue: Getting lost made us hungry! So, (8) _____ , we only saw the last part of the game.

reading

A Read the two anecdotes about strange weather events. Then write brief summaries of them.

Susan's strange weather event was _____

_____

Elena's strange weather event was _____

_____

Wacky Weather Stories

Last summer, I was working at home on a sunny day. For some reason I had gone around to the front of the house to get something. As I did, I felt drops of rain on my face, which soon developed into a very heavy rain shower. A few minutes later, I went to the back of the house and realized that it was not raining at all there. It was raining only at the front of the house and not at the back. I stood in the hallway and looked one way – heavy rain – and the other way – sunny and dry. After a few minutes, the rain stopped entirely. Up until then, I'd never seen such strange weather.
– Susan, United States

One spring day, I was sitting in the living room of my farmhouse in Uruguay watching TV. My aunt had made some lunch for me, but before that she had been ironing clothes. I was just about to get up from the sofa when suddenly a ball of fire the size of a soccer ball flew through the open kitchen window. About two seconds later, it disappeared under the front door and there was a terrible smell in the air. The TV and many electrical outlets in the house burned, as did the electric iron, and the kitchen wall was opened up by a big crack. I didn't know what had happened until someone told me that the house had been hit by a *centella*, which is the Spanish word for thunderbolt.
– Elena, Uruguay

B Check (✓) the sentences that apply to each person's story.

	Susan	Elena
1. As soon as she went to the front of the house, it started raining.	☐	☐
2. She experienced a strange weather event.	☐	☐
3. A *centella* passed through her house.	☐	☐
4. It was raining and the sun was shining at the same time.	☐	☐
5. She noticed a bad smell afterward.	☐	☐
6. She didn't know what had happened until someone told her.	☐	☐

7 The information age

1 vocabulary

Use the words and phrases in the box to complete the sentences.

| blog | hot spot | podcasts | virus |
| download | instant messaging | spyware | webcam |

1. Cosmic Café is a _____ hot spot _____ where people with laptops can use the Internet.

2. It's easy to _____ pictures from the Internet to a computer.

3. Now that I have a _____, I can send live video to my friends.

4. Al's computer crashed when he opened an e-mail that had a _____.

5. Cal has opinions about the environment that he posts on his _____.

6. Even though I moved, I still listen to _____ of my favorite hometown radio station online.

7. _____ is a popular way for teens to talk or chat on the Internet.

8. I hate websites that use _____ to gather information about me when I surf the Internet.

2 grammar

One of the underlined words in each sentence is a mistake. Circle it and write the correct word in the blank.

1. In the near future, satellite radio will (been) listened to by more and more people in their cars. _____ be _____

2. Cell phones are being using by people of all ages, not just teens. _____

3. Medical data has going to be accessed online by both doctors and patients. _____

4. More MP3s have be bought this year than ever before. _____

5. All laptops in the store has being priced to sell quickly. _____

6. More and more TV shows having been made available as podcasts. _____

7. Increasingly, photos will be post by people on their own websites. _____

8. Cell phones are going to been designed with even more features. _____

vocabulary

Circle the connectors that best complete each sentence.

1. Nat dropped his cell phone on the sidewalk yesterday. *Nevertheless /*(*As a result,*) it doesn't work anymore.

2. Parents must monitor the websites their children visit. *Additionally / On the other hand,* they need to talk to their children about Internet safety.

3. Cell phones are getting smaller. Some, *for instance / likewise,* weigh only 3.3 ounces and are less than half an inch thick.

4. Penny switched Internet service providers to save money. *Furthermore / In fact,* she's now spending $15 less each month.

5. I really don't like talking on my cell phone. *Similarly / On the other hand,* it's important to have a cell phone in case of an emergency.

6. Technology is becoming more user friendly. *For example / Therefore,* my 10-year-old daughter programmed my new digital camera by herself!

grammar

Use the passive of the present continuous and your own information to complete the sentences.

1. Blogs *are being written by just about everybody these days!*

2. An increasing number of cell phones with special features _____

3. Many online college and university classes _____

4 Some spyware _____

5. More and more radio and news podcasts _____

5

writing

A Read the blog post and underline examples you see of these things.

| informal language | title | opinions | questions | dates and times |

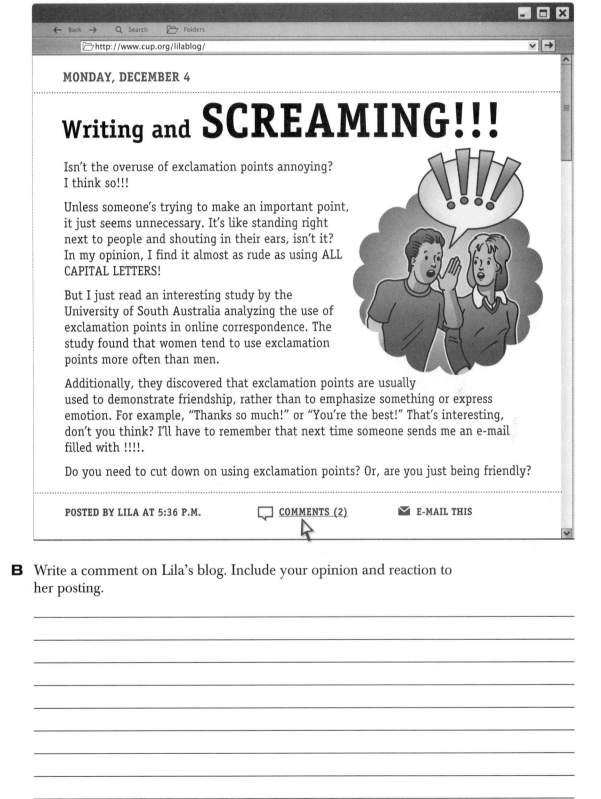

MONDAY, DECEMBER 4

Writing and SCREAMING!!!

Isn't the overuse of exclamation points annoying?
I think so!!!

Unless someone's trying to make an important point, it just seems unnecessary. It's like standing right next to people and shouting in their ears, isn't it? In my opinion, I find it almost as rude as using ALL CAPITAL LETTERS!

But I just read an interesting study by the University of South Australia analyzing the use of exclamation points in online correspondence. The study found that women tend to use exclamation points more often than men.

Additionally, they discovered that exclamation points are usually used to demonstrate friendship, rather than to emphasize something or express emotion. For example, "Thanks so much!" or "You're the best!" That's interesting, don't you think? I'll have to remember that next time someone sends me an e-mail filled with !!!!.

Do you need to cut down on using exclamation points? Or, are you just being friendly?

POSTED BY LILA AT 5:36 P.M.   💬 COMMENTS (2)   ✉ E-MAIL THIS

B Write a comment on Lila's blog. Include your opinion and reaction to her posting.

_____

_____

_____

_____

_____

_____

_____

_____

_____

_____

vocabulary

1 Use the words and phrases in the box to complete the sentences.

billboard	infomercial	pop-up ad	telemarketer	voice mail
crawl	neon signs	spam	text-messaging	

1. I saw an ad for my favorite soda on a huge ____billboard____ on the highway.
2. An _____ is a long commercial that's like a real TV show.
3. When I get a phone call at dinner, I know it's a _____ .
4. The _____ at the bottom of the TV screen said a storm is coming.
5. If I'm not home, leave a message on my _____ .
6. I hate when I'm on the Internet and a _____ interrupts me.
7. Some _____ are quite beautiful when they are lit up at night.
8. Most of the e-mail I get is _____ .
9. I hate talking on my cell phone in public, so I prefer _____ .

grammar

2 Complete these negative questions or tag questions with *isn't, doesn't, wouldn't, shouldn't,* or *don't*.

1. __Don't__ you think that there are lots of great cooking sites on the Internet?
2. _____ it be terrific if telemarketers couldn't call after 5:00 P.M.?
3. _____ it strange that no one has sent me any e-mail today?
4. _____ Sheila register online for classes soon before they fill up?
5. _____ it seem like whenever you check your e-mail it's all spam?
6. Computer viruses are getting more sophisticated, _____ you think?
7. It's almost midnight. It's too late to send a text message, _____ it?

3

grammar

Find another way to write the sentences using the words given. More than one answer is possible.

1. It's amazing how much time someone can waste surfing the Internet.   (isn't)

   Isn't it amazing how much time someone can waste surfing the Internet? /
   It's amazing how much time someone can waste surfing the Internet, isn't it?

2. It would be great to download all my favorite TV programs.   (wouldn't)

   _____

3. Students should try to avoid sending text messages during class.   (shouldn't)

   _____

4. It seems like new technology is being invented every day.   (doesn't)

   _____

5. It's annoying that some banner ads make Web pages load so slowly.   (isn't)

   _____

6. It's interesting how some bus wraps cover an entire bus.   (don't you think)

   _____

4

grammar

Write negative questions or tag questions about the Internet. Choose from problems in the box or use your own ideas.

going shopping online
looking for a job
making a doctor's appointment
paying bills
planning a vacation
reading the news

1. _It's convenient to shop for things like clothing and books online, isn't it?_

2. _____

   _____

3. _____

   _____

4. _____

   _____

5

reading

A Read the blog post. Find the boldfaced words that match these definitions.

1. deserving to be laughed at ___ridiculous___
2. pocket-sized computing devices _____
3. again and again without stopping _____
4. making you feel calm _____
5. a ringing sound _____

Are You Tech Obsessed?

Tuesday, February 2

I suppose most of us have a love-hate relationship with technology, but for some people it goes beyond healthy admiration. Take this quiz about tech obsession. How many of these are true for you?

1. When you're online, do you forget to drink, eat, use the restroom, or sleep? In South Korea, a man died in front of his computer after playing online games **continuously** for ten days!

2. Do you collect **ridiculous** accessories for your cell phone or MP3 player like those lights that start flashing for incoming calls?

3. Do you check your e-mail on Sunday at 3 a.m.?

4. Do you know your friends by their online handles rather than their real names?

5. Does your favorite song go "beep"? Tech-obsessed people find the start-up noises of their computers and the **chime** of incoming mail oddly **soothing.**

6. Do you answer your cell phone when you're out on a date, at a movie, at a ballgame, at a restaurant, or anywhere?

7. Do you change your cell phone's outfits? Are you like the millions of other tech obsessed who like putting their cell phones, MP3 players, laptops, or **handhelds** into their latest covers?

8. Do you speak in technical language? For example, you might say about a new friend, "I bookmarked him after we met in English class."

This quiz was pretty funny, don't you think? Unfortunately, I answered "yes" to seven of them! How about you? Are you tech obsessed like me?

Posted by Walker White at 5:36 p.m.   Comments (8)

B Read the statements. Do you think the author of the article would say these behaviors were obsessive or not obsessive? Check (✓) the correct answer.

	Obsessive	Not obsessive
1. You go online for about 30 minutes at a time.	☐	☑
2. People don't often understand you because you use a lot of technical words.	☐	☐
3. You forget to eat because you're chatting online.	☐	☐
4. You rarely buy tech gadgets or accessories.	☐	☐
5. You go online even when you're really sick.	☐	☐
6. You don't know your friends' online names without looking them up.	☐	☐

1

grammar

Do you agree (A) or disagree (D) with these statements? Check (✓) your answer. Then explain your reason.

	A	D
1. A person with good cooking skills would make a good restaurant owner.	✓	☐

A person with good cooking skills might make a good
restaurant owner, but you also need good business skills.

2. Someone planning to be a scientist doesn't need to write well. ☐ ☐

_____

_____

3. A person looking for a job should have a good sense of humor. ☐ ☐

_____

_____

4. Someone planning to work with kids needs to have patience. ☐ ☐

_____

_____

2

grammar

Reduce each relative clause. Then complete the sentences with your own ideas.

1. A person who is living on a tight budget . . .

   A person living on a tight budget shouldn't eat out too often.

2. Anyone who is interested in becoming a doctor . . .

   _____

3. Someone who is considering becoming an artist . . .

   _____

4. People who are able to work at home . . .

   _____

5. A supervisor who has too much work to do . . .

   _____

6. Anyone who is required to take a foreign language in school . . .

   _____

3

vocabulary

A Which of the words are nouns (*N*) and which are adjectives (*A*)? Write the correct letter.

1. curiosity <u>N</u>
2. decisive ____
3. determined ____
4. discipline ____
5. innovative ____
6. knowledgeable ____
7. motivation ____
8. originality ____
9. passion ____
10. patient ____
11. perceptive ____
12. resourceful ____

B Now write sentences about these people using the words above.

1. business executive <u>A person with innovative ideas might make a good</u> <u>business executive.</u>

2. Web designer _____
_____

3. counselor _____
_____

4. attorney _____
_____

4

grammar

What qualities are needed to do these jobs? Use reduced relative clauses in your answers.

clown

landscaper

architect

1. A person considering becoming a clown needs to be _____ _____ _____

2. _____ _____ _____ _____

3. _____ _____ _____ _____

writing

A Read the composition. Check (✓) the word or words you would use to describe this person.

☐ determined   ☐ resourceful   ☐ original   ☐ curious

    If you drive a car, this has probably happened to you, but I certainly never thought it would happen to me. However, it did! A few months ago, I had just gotten out of my car and locked the door when I realized that my keys were still in the car. To make matters worse, I had left the engine running! I didn't have a spare key and had no idea what to do. I was about to call the police when I got an idea. I noticed that I had left the window open just a little bit. I had just picked up some shirts from the cleaner's, so I took one off a hanger and took the hanger apart. I straightened it out and made a small hook at the end of the hanger, and then I pushed the hook through the opening in the window. After several tries, I was able to get the hook around the lock, pull it up, and open the door. Although I felt pleased with myself for getting the door open, I also felt like a fool for getting into that situation in the first place. Right away, I went out and got two sets of spare keys made. I taped one set of keys under the car, and I gave the other set to a friend for safekeeping. I want to make sure that I'm prepared if this ever happens again!

B Read the composition again. Write a Ⓟ where you think each new paragraph should begin.

C Write a three-paragraph composition about a problem you actually had or imagine you might have. How did you or would you solve the problem?

    If you _____ , this probably has happened to you, but I certainly never thought it would happen to me. Recently,

_____

_____

    I was about to _____ when I got an idea.

_____

_____

_____

    Later, _____

_____

_____

vocabulary

Circle the word that best completes each sentence.

1. Seat belts did not protect car passengers enough, which is why researchers *solved* /(*found*) *made* a safer solution: air bags for cars.

2. You need to *organize* / *explore* / *solve* your information before you present it to your colleagues. Otherwise, they won't understand it.

3. Our report *explored* / *made* / *solved* several possibilities for increasing worker efficiency.

4. The ground technicians *organized* / *found* / *made* a serious problem with one of the engines, which is why the plane was delayed.

5. It's important to consider many solutions when you are *organizing* / *making* / *analyzing* a problem.

6. Our science experiment didn't work. We *solved* / *explored* / *made* a mistake in the calculations.

grammar

Read the conversation. Find the mistakes in the underlined sentences, and rewrite them so that they are correct.

A: Why are we leaving so early? The meeting doesn't start for another 30 minutes!

B: At this time of day, the traffic is terrible! <u>It moves only at about 20 miles an hour, that means we need to leave now.</u>

A: Why don't we go by public transportation?

B: <u>The buses are even slower which is why people avoid using them.</u>

A: Then how about walking? <u>The office is a short distance from here, which it means that it shouldn't take long.</u>

B: <u>Yes, but then you'll have to breathe in the exhaust fumes from all the cars, it is why there are so few pedestrians.</u>

1. It moves only at about 20 miles an hour, which means (that) we need to leave now.

2. _____

3. _____

4. _____

grammar

Write sentences about these topics. Use non-defining relative clauses beginning with *which is why* or *which means (that)*.

the common cold   *ATM*   *laptop computer*   *pollution*

1. There is no cure for the common cold, <u>which is why researchers are working</u> <u>to find one.</u>

2. ATM machines have become more available, _____
   _____

3. Laptop computers are easy to carry anywhere, _____
   _____

4. Pollution has become a major problem in many cities, _____
   _____

grammar

Combine the sentences with non-defining relative clauses beginning with *which is why* or *which means (that)*.

1. People feel the need to keep in touch. Cell phones have become popular.
   <u>People feel the need to keep in touch, which is why cell phones have</u>
   <u>become popular.</u>

2. New diseases are being discovered all the time. Researchers have to work even harder.
   _____

3. People like listening to music on the go. MP3 players have become popular.
   _____

4. Traffic congestion is becoming a major problem in cities. New types of public transportation will have to be developed.
   _____

5. Reality TV shows are cheap and easy to produce. There are fewer comedy and drama shows on television.
   _____

5 **A** What does *basics* mean in the title "Back to Basics"? Read the article and check (✓) the correct answer.

reading

☐ donating money to schools
☐ the name of a computer program
☐ reading, writing, and mathematics

Back to Basics

My friend Mike was shaking his head in disbelief. "That young woman who just waited on me," he said, indicating an employee of the fast-food restaurant where we were eating, "had to call someone over to help her make change. The cash register showed her I needed 99 cents, but she couldn't figure out how to count out the coins." I understood Mike's concern. What we have done in this country, although unintentionally, is to create several generations of individuals most of whom have no idea how to reason; how to do simple mathematical procedures; how to do research; or, finally, how to be creative. The reason for this is our overuse of information technology: video games, television, VCRs, digital watches, calculators, and computers. Information technology feeds us information without requiring us to think about it. Technology lets us perform operations without understanding them.

It is time we took a hard look at an educational system that teaches our children only how to push buttons. Our kids can't tell time if the clock has hands. They can use calculators, but they cannot add, subtract, divide, or multiply. Video games have replaced active, imaginative play. Although most of them are technically literate, they choose not to read. They are only

accustomed to television and movies, which is why they cannot use their imaginations to stay interested in a book.

It is not enough to recognize that a problem exists. What we need is a solution. The one I offer is simple to suggest, but may be impossible to implement: We must unplug our children. If we don't, they will never learn how to solve problems. They will never learn even basic reasoning skills and will certainly not develop creativity. Instead of filling classrooms with electronics, let's concentrate on good old-fashioned literacy – reading books. Students must be taught not to perform computer operations by rote, but to figure and reason for themselves. They must see how things work and how processes lead to results. They must also stretch their imaginations.

B Read the article again. For each pair of sentences, check the one that the author would agree with.

1. ☐ a. Children depend on calculators too much.
   ☐ b. Children should learn to use calculators at school.

2. ☐ a. Many children are illiterate.
   ☐ b. Many children do not like to read.

3. ☐ a. Children must watch less TV and learn basic skills.
   ☐ b. Children who learn basic skills will not learn to be creative.

4. ☐ a. Children should never use information technology.
   ☐ b. Children should learn how things work.

grammar

Circle the expression that best completes each sentence.

1. (*Unlike*) / *While* many Americans, people in my country do not watch a lot of TV.

2. *In contrast to* / *While* many of my friends eat meat, I'm a vegetarian.

3. Monica is a typical teenager, *unlike* / *except for the fact that* she likes to get up early in the morning.

4. *Unlike* / *While* people who shower in the morning, I take one at night.

5. I'm similar to people my age, *while* / *except that* I don't live at home.

6. *Unlike* / *While* most of my classmates, I prefer spending time with my grandparents to going out with people my own age.

7. Students in my country are just like other kids, *unlike* / *except that* we sometimes have to go to school on Saturdays.

8. I like all kinds of music, *except for* / *except that* hard rock music.

vocabulary

Use the words and phrases in the box to complete the sentences.

amenable to
conform to
conservative
fit in
follows the crowd
make waves
rebels against
unconventional

1. Emma _____fit in_____ easily at her new school and made lots of friends.

2. I don't mind working overtime. I'm actually _____ it.

3. Neil likes to do his own thing. He doesn't _____ other people's ideas.

4. Sam doesn't like people who tell him what to do. He _____ authority.

5. My town is very resistant to change. It's quite _____ .

6. Sadie hates to bring attention to herself. She doesn't like to _____ .

7. Jake has _____ ideas about his work. He tries to be original.

8. My teenage daughter usually _____ when it comes to clothing. She likes to dress exactly like her friends.

3

grammar

Read these descriptions of people. Who are you similar to or different from? Write sentences using *unlike*, *while*, *in contrast to*, *except that*, *except for*, and *except for the fact that*.

What are you like?

I am a college sophomore, and my major is English literature. My interests include tennis, reading, and travel. I enjoy exploring new places – especially places few people visit.

– Kim

Hi! I love music of all kinds, and I play drums in a rock band. I love loud music – the louder the better. I'm interested in musical instruments, and I enjoy collecting them.

– Maria

I am a 25-year-old computer science student. I am very interested in technology and soccer. I love building computers in my spare time.

– Donald

Do you like visiting historical sites? Do you enjoy reading books about history? I do. I am 23 and an accountant, but my real passion is history. I also enjoy collecting rare coins.

– Luis

1. <u>I have a lot in common with Kim, except that I don't like sports.</u>

2. _____

3. _____

4. _____

writing

A Read these paragraphs and answer the questions.

> **M**ore and more Americans are living alone. While some live alone because of divorce or the death of a partner, even more people live alone because they choose to. According to a recent U.S. census, 25% of all households in the U.S. are made up of just one person. This is a dramatic change from the extended families of just a couple of generations ago.

1. What is the topic sentence?

   _____

2. What reasons are given to support the topic sentence?

   _____

   _____

3. What fact is given to support the topic sentence?

   _____

> **T**he typical American living alone is neither old nor lonely. In fact, a quarter of the 23 million single people in the U.S. are under the age of 35. The majority of these people have chosen to live alone. They are responding to decreasing social pressure to get married and have a family.

4. What is the topic sentence?

   _____

5. What fact is given to support the topic sentence?

   _____

   _____

6. What reasons are given to support the topic sentence?

   _____

   _____

B Choose the topic sentence below that you like best. Then add at least four supporting statements to make a complete paragraph.

> It is *unusual / typical* for young people in my country to live alone.
> It is *easy / difficult* to buy a house in my country.

_____

_____

_____

_____

grammar Complete the diary entry with *used to*, *didn't use to*, or *would*, and the words in the box. Sometimes more than one answer is possible.

| like | listen | not be | not turn on | play | save | watch |

Sunday, March 14

I had a funny conversation with my dad the other day. He was telling me what things were like when he was a kid. First of all, there (1) <u>didn't use to be</u> any technology

like computers, MP3 players, or handheld games to entertain him. When he wanted to hear music, he (2) _____ to the radio or he (3) _____ a record on a record player. He did have a TV, but he (4) _____ it only at night. He (5) _____ the TV during the day because there were only four channels and the programs were boring in the daytime. He also said he (6) _____ reading mystery and suspense novels. He (7) _____ his allowance to buy his favorite books. I feel kind of bad for my dad – it sounds like he had a boring childhood!

vocabulary Complete the dialogue with *keep* or *stay*. Sometimes more than one answer is possible.

Lola: Mrs. Wu's English class is boring. Do you have any advice to help me _____<u>stay</u>_____ awake?

Max: Be careful! Mrs. Wu is demanding. My best advice is to _____ up with the work you need to do each day. And don't procrastinate!

Lola: That's good advice. Her assignments are long and complicated! I always worry I won't be able to _____ my grades up in her class!

Max: Even though you're stressed out, try to _____ things in perspective. Also, if you let her know that you will do what it takes to get good grades, maybe she'll help you _____ out of trouble.

Lola: That's a good idea. I'll talk to Mrs. Wu tomorrow. And I'll _____ in touch with you to let you know how things go.

3

grammar

Rewrite each sentence using the past habitual with *used to* or *would*. If there are two possibilities, write them.

1. James was a very good chess player when he was younger.

   <u>James used to be a very good chess player when he was younger.</u>

2. In college, my friends and I studied for our tests together at the library.

   _____

3. I always asked my older sister for help with my science homework.

   _____

4. My English teacher didn't assign work over holidays or long weekends.

   _____

5. Rowan lived in an apartment near the university.

   _____

6. Carrie wrote e-mails to her mom every day when she went away to school.

   _____

4

grammar

Complete the sentences with information that is true for you.

1. Three years ago, I _____<u>used to</u>_____ live <u>in a very small apartment on a noisy</u> <u>city street.</u>_____

2. Last summer, my friends and I _____
   _____
   _____
   _____

3. When I was younger, _____ go to _____
   _____
   _____

4. I _____ have trouble in _____ class because
   _____

5. My favorite teacher was _____ . He / She _____
   _____

6. When I was first learning English, I _____
   _____

A Read the article quickly to find the answers to the questions.

1. What percentage of Americans live alone? _____

2. Who makes up the growing number of Americans living alone? _____

The Joy of Living Alone

More and more Americans are living alone. While some live alone because of divorce or the death of a partner, even more people live alone because they choose to. According to a recent U.S. census, 25% of all households in the U.S. are made up of just one person. This is a dramatic change from the extended families of just a couple of generations ago.

The typical American living alone is neither old nor lonely. In fact, a quarter of the 23 million single people in the U.S. are under the age of 35. The majority of these people have chosen to live alone. They are responding to decreasing social pressure to get married and have a family.

It's now socially acceptable, even chic, to live alone. As people get better jobs and become financially independent, it becomes possible for them to maintain a one-person household. The growing number of women with good jobs has done much to increase the number of people living alone. However, people who do get married are marrying at a later age and divorcing more often.

The number one reason given by most people for living alone is that they simply enjoy doing what they want when they want to do it. "Living alone is a luxury," says Nina Hagiwara, 38. "Once you do it, you can't ever go back to living with others." David de Baca, 46, agrees. He says, "I like living by myself."

Children think that being grown up means being able to do exactly as they please. It seems that many grown-ups today are living out that childhood dream. The chance to discover whether that freedom is as wonderful as it sounds is a chance more and more Americans are taking.

B Read the article again. Are the statements true or false? Check (✓) the correct answer. Then rewrite the false statements to make them true.

	True	False
1. The number of one-person households has not changed over the years.	☐	☐
_____		
2. There's more pressure to get married these days.	☐	☐
_____		
3. People can maintain one-person households because they receive money from their parents.	☐	☐
_____		
4. People who marry are getting married younger.	☐	☐
_____		
5. Many adults are discovering the freedom of living alone.	☐	☐
_____		

10 The art of complaining

1

grammar

Use the phrases in the box to complete the sentences.

people who make noise when they eat	water dripping in the sink
how complicated it is to use	who honk their horns all the time
when my favorite show is interrupted by a news bulletin	waiting a long time to be seated
why people push in front of me in line	

1. The thing that really bothers me at the dinner table is . . .

   The thing that really bothers me at the dinner table is people who make noise when they eat.

2. When I'm trying to sleep at night, something that irks me is . . .

   _____

3. One thing I can't understand in the supermarket is . . .

   _____

4. The thing that really irritates me when I go to a restaurant is . . .

   _____

5. I can't stand drivers . . .

   _____

6. Something that bothers me about my new MP3 player is . . .

   _____

7. When I'm watching TV, one thing that bugs me is . . .

   _____

2

grammar

Write sentences about things that irritate you. Use information from Exercise 1.

1. *The thing that really irritates me when I go to a restaurant is high prices for food that doesn't taste very good.*

2. _____

   _____

3. _____

   _____

4. _____

   _____

3
grammar

Use relative clauses and noun clauses to write about everyday annoyances in these places.

traffic   **in the park**   **in the library**   **on the subway**

1. _The thing that annoys me about traffic is drivers who follow too closely._

2. _____

3. _____

4. _____

4
vocabulary

Circle the word that best completes each sentence.

1. The thing that (*makes*)/ *gets* / *drives* my blood boil is when my sister borrows my clothes.

2. Something that *makes* / *gets* / *drives* me up the wall is when I have to wait on a long line to buy one or two items.

3. One thing that *makes* / *gets* / *drives* me down is when it rains on the weekend.

4. When I'm reading, one thing that *makes* / *gets* / *drives* my goat is people talking loudly.

5. The one thing that *makes* / *gets* / *drives* under my skin is when someone's cell phone rings during a movie or play.

6. When I'm talking to someone, the thing that *makes* / *gets* / *drives* on my nerves is when he or she keeps interrupting me.

7. Telemarketers calling during dinner *makes* / *gets* / *drives* me crazy.

8. One thing my brother does that *makes* / *gets* / *drives* under my skin is when he doesn't clean up the kitchen after he cooks a meal.

5

A Read the letter of complaint and number the paragraphs in a logical order.

February 2, 2008

Dear Sir or Madam,

_____ The radio I received, a typical AM/FM model, is not the one I ordered. The model number on this radio is F146. The price of the radio is the same as the one I ordered, but it is obviously a different model.

_____ Please send me the correct radio or the full refund no later than February 16th. I like the products your company sells, and I would like to be able to order them in the future with the same confidence as in the past. I look forward to hearing from you soon.

_____ Please send the radio I ordered, model G146, and refund $18.77, the cost of insuring and shipping the wrong radio (copy of receipt enclosed). If model G146 is not available, please issue a full refund, including all shipping costs I have paid.

_____ Three weeks ago, I ordered a radio from your catalog by telephone. It was a shortwave radio, model number G146.

Sincerely,
Emily Goldstein
egoldstein@cup.org

B Now use the numbers you wrote for the paragraphs above to answer these questions. In which paragraph does the writer . . .

a. explain the problem in detail? _____   c. give a precise description of the product? _____

b. give a deadline? _____   d. explain what she wants? _____

C Write your own letter of complaint about a problem regarding something you bought recently.

Dear _____ ,

_____

_____

_____

_____

_____

_____

_____

_____

_____

1

grammar

Write *S* for a simple indirect question and *C* for a complex indirect question.

_S_ 1. I want to find out how to use less fat in my cooking.

____ 2. Why people aren't concerned about the crime rate is a mystery to me.

____ 3. I wonder if other people are concerned about the pollution problems in our city.

____ 4. The thing I don't get is why food prices are so high.

____ 5. One of my concerns is whether I will be able to afford a new car.

____ 6. I'd like to know if the weather will be nice this weekend.

____ 7. How kids can listen to such loud music is something I can't understand.

____ 8. I want to know when a cure for the common cold will be discovered.

2

grammar

Use the words in parentheses to rewrite the questions.

1. Why are the trains running so slowly?   (. . . is a mystery to me.)
   Why the trains are running so slowly is a mystery to me.

2. Will there be cheaper health care for employees?   (One of my concerns . . .)
   _____

3. Why do I get so much junk mail?   (. . . is beyond me.)
   _____

4. How can you eat so much and not gain weight?   (What I don't get . . .)
   _____

5. Who should I call if I don't get my plane tickets on time?   (I wonder . . .)
   _____

6. Will politicians do more to help the environment?   (I'd like to know . . .)
   _____

7. Why don't people turn off their cell phones when they're at the movies?
   (. . . is something I can't understand.)
   _____

8. Why can't everyone just get along?   (. . . is the thing that concerns me.)
   _____

9. Why do I get a cold every summer?   (. . . is a mystery to me.)
   _____

3

vocabulary

Circle the word that best completes each sentence.

1. Lena was (*infuriated*)/*insulted* when she missed her flight due to the traffic jam.

2. John was terribly *irritated / saddened* when his grandmother died.

3. Vicky was *baffled / depressed* when the forecast called for rain on her wedding.

4. The players on the football team were *humiliated / insulted* when they lost the championship game by 50 points.

5. We were absolutely *demoralized / stunned* when we found out we had the winning lottery ticket.

6. Chiang lost the directions for his clock radio, so now he is completely *baffled / insulted* about how to reset the time.

4

grammar

Write two sentences about problems in your city. Choose from the topics below or use ideas of your own.

| parking | transportation | sanitation |

1. I don't know why bus service is so infrequent. It's almost impossible to get to work on time.

2. It's beyond me _____

_____

3. I wonder _____

_____

4. My big concern _____

_____

reading

A Read the article quickly. Check (✓) the word or words you think best describe how the people quoted on the complaint website feel.

☐ frustrated   ☐ baffled   ☐ humiliated   ☐ irritated   ☐ demoralized

Complaining ⊙NLINE

Websites designed especially for complaining are hardly **unique** these days. If you have a complaint, there are hundreds of sites that allow you to **get it off your chest**. Sites exist for complaining about such things as defective products, government inefficiency, and offensive advertising. There are even sites where you can complain about anything that **bugs** you, including love, family, or just the weather. These websites won't actually do anything about your problem; they just let you **blow off steam**. Here's a sampling of complaints people have written:

▶ Something that really irks me is pencils! They need to be sharpened after every page you write. And then don't you hate it when they start to make a scratching noise?

▶ Have you ever noticed that in most schools you have chairs with armrests to write on attached to the right-hand side of the chair only? I wonder if there are desks for left-handed people?

It's very uncomfortable for us "lefties" to use these desks made for right-handed people!

▶ I **see red** every time I get my credit card bill from the bank. There's always a check for a large amount attached with an invitation to sign it and spend it on "anything I want." I have enough **sense** to rip it up and throw it away, but I bet a lot of people don't. They don't realize that when they use the "free" check, the expense gets put on their credit card bill. Boy, they must be stunned when they get that bill! I think that banks shouldn't be **tempting** people with those checks.

▶ It isn't fair that the U.S. **dominates** the Internet! I go to fill in a request for a catalog or a prize or a free offer, and I find it's limited to residents of the U.S. I live outside the U.S., and it's frustrating!

▶ My pet peeve is people who complain on this site! What good does it do anyway? Come on, everyone! Grow up! **Get over it!**

B Read the article again to find the meaning of the boldfaced words or phrases. Write the words next to their definitions.

1. express your anger ___blow off steam___

2. has the most influence _____

3. say what you want to say _____

4. get angry _____

5. intelligence _____

6. offering an attractive choice _____

7. Don't let it bother you. _____

8. like nothing else _____

9. bothers _____

LESSON A · How honest are you?

1

grammar

Complete the sentences with *unless, only if,* or *even if.*

1. I wouldn't interrupt my teacher _____unless_____ I had an important question.

2. I would leave the scene of a car accident _____ I knew for sure that no one was injured.

3. _____ I were really hungry, I still wouldn't take food that wasn't mine.

4. I wouldn't wear an ugly sweater someone had given me _____ I knew I'd see that person that day. It's important to show you appreciate people's gifts.

5. I would take credit for a co-worker's idea _____ I knew he or she wouldn't mind.

6. _____ I didn't like my brother's new wife, I'd still be nice to her.

2

vocabulary

Circle the correct words to complete these sentences.

1. Min Hee won't mind if we rewrite parts of her article. She's pretty (agreeable)/ *legal* to change.

2. It's *unfair / untrustworthy* that Mrs. Gomez only blamed Lydia for the accident. Terry was responsible for the accident too.

3. Mark wasn't being *honest / acceptable* when he said he liked my new shoes.

4. I can't believe Brianna wasn't fired from her job. Her *trustworthy / unscrupulous* business practices have cost this company thousands of dollars.

5. Stephanie is a good choice for club treasurer. She's good with money, and she's quite *disagreeable / responsible.*

6. In many places, it's *approving / illegal* to use a handheld cell phone and drive at the same time.

3 *grammar*

Respond to what the first speaker says in each of these conversations.

1. A: If I found a wallet on the street that contained a lot of money, I wouldn't try to return it.

   B: Really? I'd try to return the wallet even if _____ _____ _____

2. A: You should never give a friend your e-mail password.

   B: I would give a friend my e-mail password only if _____ _____ _____

3. A: If I heard someone spreading false information about a good friend, I wouldn't tell that friend about it.

   B: I wouldn't tell my friend about the false information unless _____ _____ _____ _____

4. A: I would always lend my best friend a lot of money if she needed it.

   B: I wouldn't lend my best friend a lot of money unless _____ _____

4 *grammar*

How do you feel about telling lies in these situations? Write sentences about them using *unless, only if,* or *even if.*

- exaggerating your qualifications on your résumé
- lying about why you were late for work
- making up a story about being too busy to see a friend
- lying about how much you were paid for something

1. I would never exaggerate my qualifications on my résumé even if it meant I wouldn't get the job.

2. _____ _____

3. _____ _____

4. _____ _____

writing

A Read this composition and check (✓) the best thesis statement.

☐ I am glad that I learned the value of work when I was young.

☐ I am thankful that I learned the value of money as a child.

☐ I feel fortunate to have learned as a child that work is fun.

_____ I grew up on a farm. We had to care for the animals morning and evening, seven days a week. Even during school vacations and on weekends there was work to do. I was paid for my work. From the age of 10, I was paid $1 an hour.

Because of this, I learned how to save and budget money. When I was only 11, I saved enough to buy a ten-speed bicycle. In high school, I took a job in a nearby town during the summer to save money for college. I learned how to manage money at an early age.

I also learned the satisfaction of work well done. The young animals were my responsibility. Most farmers had problems with their calves frequently getting sick. I was proud that my calves were usually healthy. I loved it when the whole family worked together to get a field of hay into the barn before a rainstorm. It was exciting when we jumped out of bed in the middle of the night to chase the cows back into the field after they'd escaped through a broken fence. Doing hard work at an early age taught me how rewarding it can be. These experiences taught me confidence and self-discipline.

B Check (✓) the values you learned growing up. Then fill in the chart.

☐ courage   ☐ forgiveness   ☐ loyalty
☐ determination ☐ honesty   ☐ patience
☐ discipline   ☐ kindness   ☐ politeness

Value I learned	How I learned it

C Now write a thesis statement based on one of the values you checked above.

I'm glad that I learned _____

_____

_____

1

grammar

Complete the sentences with the correct form of the verbs in parentheses.

1. Jay: I'm taking a French class at the community college.

   Meryl: I wish I _____ had _____ more time so I could learn a second language. (have)

2. Diego: I have to study tonight.

   Jim: If you _____ yesterday, you would have been able to go to the concert with me tonight! (study)

3. Kate: If only our neighbor _____ his music quieter at night! (play)

   Derek: I know. I haven't had a good night of sleep since he moved in!

4. Micah: The boss is going to be upset when he sees what you've done.

   Julie: It's true. If I had been careful, I _____ my drink on my computer. (not spill)

5. Albin: You look exhausted. Why don't you stop working for a few minutes?

   Lily: I wish I _____ a break, but I have too much to do! (take)

2

grammar

Write sentences with wishes and regrets about the illustration. Use the first person and phrases in the box.

| forget my umbrella | watch the weather report |
| wear my raincoat | find a taxi |

1. <u>I wish I hadn't forgotten my umbrella.</u>

   _____

2. _____

   _____

3. _____

   _____

4. _____

   _____

3

vocabulary

Complete these sentences with the words from the box.

| compassionate | generous | resilient | selfish |
| discreet | indifference | respect | tolerance |

1. Even though Mr. Soto gave a _____generous_____ donation to the library fund, he wishes he could have given more.

2. If I had been more _____ , Jerry wouldn't have found out about her surprise birthday party.

3. Don't be late for your appointment with Ms. Benson. She doesn't have much _____ for tardiness.

4. We lost all _____ for Ben when he lied about who broke the computer.

5. If only more people would be _____ toward the homeless.

6. Gina is pretty _____ . Even though she lost the singing competition, she'll be ready to sing again tomorrow.

7. George's _____ about global warming really bothers me.

8. Brad is so _____ . He only thinks about how things affect him.

4

grammar

Write one sentence with a wish about the present or future and one sentence with a regret about the past.

1. Tim stopped at a pay phone to call a friend. He put his wallet down next to the phone for a moment. When he went to pick it up, the wallet was gone! There was $100 in the wallet.

   Tim wishes he could _find his wallet._____

   Tim wishes he hadn't _____

2. Laura had a 5:00 flight. She left her house at 3:45 and boarded a bus for the airport. Unfortunately, the bus was late. She missed her flight.

   _____

   _____

3. Charles was planning to study for four hours for his driver's test the next day. He went to the movies with his friend instead and studied for only 20 minutes. He failed the test.

   _____

   _____

4. Maxine quit going to college in her junior year. She planned to take one year off to travel and then go back to school. That was five years ago.

   _____

   _____

5

reading

A Read the article quickly and check (✓) what kind of website this is.

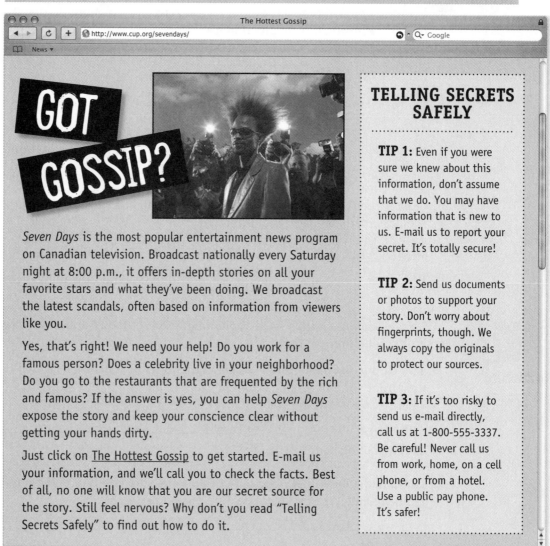

The Hottest Gossip

http://www.cup.org/sevendays/

News ▼

GOT GOSSIP?

Seven Days is the most popular entertainment news program on Canadian television. Broadcast nationally every Saturday night at 8:00 p.m., it offers in-depth stories on all your favorite stars and what they've been doing. We broadcast the latest scandals, often based on information from viewers like you.

Yes, that's right! We need your help! Do you work for a famous person? Does a celebrity live in your neighborhood? Do you go to the restaurants that are frequented by the rich and famous? If the answer is yes, you can help *Seven Days* expose the story and keep your conscience clear without getting your hands dirty.

Just click on <u>The Hottest Gossip</u> to get started. E-mail us your information, and we'll call you to check the facts. Best of all, no one will know that you are our secret source for the story. Still feel nervous? Why don't you read "Telling Secrets Safely" to find out how to do it.

TELLING SECRETS SAFELY

TIP 1: Even if you were sure we knew about this information, don't assume that we do. You may have information that is new to us. E-mail us to report your secret. It's totally secure!

TIP 2: Send us documents or photos to support your story. Don't worry about fingerprints, though. We always copy the originals to protect our sources.

TIP 3: If it's too risky to send us e-mail directly, call us at 1-800-555-3337. Be careful! Never call us from work, home, on a cell phone, or from a hotel. Use a public pay phone. It's safer!

B Read the article again. Complete these tips given by *Seven Days*.

1. You should click on <u>The Hottest Gossip</u> to get _____

2. You should send us _____ to _____

3. You shouldn't worry about _____ because we always _____

    _____

4. You should never call us _____

C Which is *not* a concern of the staff at *Seven Days*? Check (✓) the correct answer.

1

grammar

Look at the timeline of twins Max and Leila Butler's lives. Are the sentences true or false? Check (✓) the correct answer. Then rewrite the false sentences to make them true.

Max and Leila's timeline

January 2010 born

February 2012 learn to talk

August 2032 leave on a trip around the world

start to walk **January 2011**

go to school for the first time **September 2015**

graduate from college **June 2032**

	True	False
1. By January 2011, Max and Leila will have been walking for six months already.	☐	☑

By January 2011, Max and Leila will be starting to walk.
_____

| 2. By May 2012, they already will have learned to talk. | ☐ | ☐ |

_____
_____

| 3. By September 2015, they will have been attending school for only two months. | ☐ | ☐ |

_____
_____

| 4. By June 2029, they will have graduated from high school and college. | ☐ | ☐ |

_____
_____

| 5. It's now August 2031. By this time next year, they will have started traveling around the world. | ☐ | ☐ |

_____
_____

| 6. By August 2034, they will have been traveling for two years. | ☐ | ☐ |

_____
_____

2

grammar

Complete the e-mail. Use the future perfect or future perfect continuous of the verbs in parentheses.

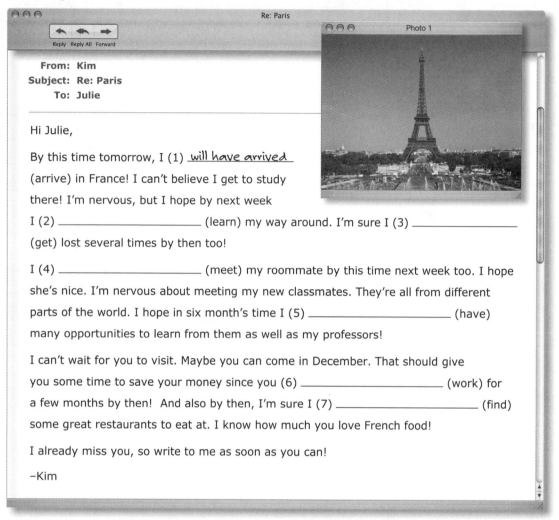

Re: Paris

Reply Reply All Forward

From: **Kim**
Subject: **Re: Paris**
To: **Julie**

Hi Julie,

By this time tomorrow, I (1) _will have arrived_ (arrive) in France! I can't believe I get to study there! I'm nervous, but I hope by next week I (2) _____ (learn) my way around. I'm sure I (3) _____ (get) lost several times by then too!

I (4) _____ (meet) my roommate by this time next week too. I hope she's nice. I'm nervous about meeting my new classmates. They're all from different parts of the world. I hope in six month's time I (5) _____ (have) many opportunities to learn from them as well as my professors!

I can't wait for you to visit. Maybe you can come in December. That should give you some time to save your money since you (6) _____ (work) for a few months by then! And also by then, I'm sure I (7) _____ (find) some great restaurants to eat at. I know how much you love French food!

I already miss you, so write to me as soon as you can!

–Kim

3

vocabulary

Complete the sentences with *about*, *in*, *of*, *on*, or *to*. Sometimes more than one answer is possible.

1. Kenji can't wait for his trip to the United States. He's looking forward __to__ visiting California and New York.

2. Before Nicole left to study abroad, she participated _____ a special training program.

3. If you have the opportunity to study abroad, don't be scared _____ taking it.

4. Michelle made friends easily after she adjusted _____ the new culture.

5. Jack couldn't stop smiling. He was excited _____ meeting the other students from his school who were chosen to study abroad in China.

6. If you want to take advantage _____ your school's study abroad programs, you should talk to your advisor.

4 **writing**

A Read the three conclusions about different summer camps for teens.
Match them with the methods used.

a. looks to the future   b. concludes with the main idea   c. summarizes the main points

_____ 1. In conclusion, the most talented and motivated young people from all over the world attend art camps every summer for creative writing, dance, film, musical theater, and even circus performance. No matter what the activity, art-camp teens are able to explore and create in fields of art that they do not have the opportunity to learn at school.

_____ 2. To sum up, adventure camp goers will meet three goals during their stay. First, students will learn skills for a lifetime of safe outdoor enjoyment. Second, they will gain experience, self-confidence, and leadership skills. Last, they will develop the proper concern for environmental preservation.

_____ 3. In brief, whether they play tennis, volleyball, or soccer at sports camps, young people will not only improve their game and get into physical shape, but they will have a great time doing it. These experiences will allow campers the chance to flourish in all aspects of their lives after the summer has ended.

B Underline the words or phrases that helped you decide on which method was used.

C Write a short composition about an activity that people enjoy where you live.
Your conclusion should contain at least one of the methods.

_____

_____

_____

_____

_____

_____

_____

_____

_____

_____

_____

_____

_____

_____

_____

_____

_____

_____

_____

grammar

Use the verbs in parentheses to complete the letter. Use mixed conditionals.

Dear Elena,

Well, I'm halfway through my tour of Peru. I'd like to say that everything is going well, but unfortunately that isn't the case. I think if I (1) __had prepared__ (prepare) a little more thoroughly, I (2) _____ (enjoy) myself a lot more right now. I guess if I (3) _____ (take) more time to research where I was going to stay, I (4) _____ (have) a better time.

My biggest mistake is that I didn't bring the right clothes. I brought all my summer clothes, and it is absolutely freezing! If I (5) _____ (bring) the right clothes, I (6) _____ (be) healthy right now. Instead, I have a terrible cold. I went to a local drugstore to get some cold medicine, but no one could understand what I wanted. I think I bought the wrong medicine. If I (7) _____ (buy) the right medicine, I (8) _____ (not sneeze) all the time! If I (9) _____ (follow) your advice about the weather and accommodations, I (10) _____ (not have) so many problems right now!

Anyway, I'll remember next time. I miss you!

Love, Sophia

grammar

Match the clauses to make conditional sentences. Write the correct letter.

1. If I had packed more carefully, _____

2. If hadn't chosen a discount airline, _____

3. If I had studied English more often, _____

4. If I had left for the airport earlier, _____

5. If I hadn't forgotten my novel, _____

a. I wouldn't be afraid to ask people for directions.

b. I wouldn't be reading a boring magazine right now.

c. I wouldn't be searching my bags for my passport.

d. I would have a nice dinner to look forward to on board.

e. I wouldn't be late for my flight!

3

vocabulary

What characteristics do you think would be most important for these people?
Write two sentences about each picture using the adjectives from the box.

culturally aware	nonconforming	open-minded	self-motivated
culturally sensitive	nonjudgmental	self-assured	self-reliant

mountain climber

businessperson abroad

1. The mountain climber has to be _____ because _____
   _____

2. If the mountain climber weren't _____ , he _____
   _____

3. The businessperson abroad should be _____
   _____

4. If the businessperson abroad weren't _____
   _____

4

grammar

Complete the sentences so they are true for you.

1. If I had been open-minded about studying abroad in college, I would have
   much more international experience on my résumé.

2. If I had been self-assured when _____ ,
   I _____

3. If I had been more of a self-starter when I was younger, I _____
   _____

4. If I hadn't been open minded about _____ ,
   I _____

A Read the article quickly. Check (✓) the tips that are mentioned.

☐ call your friends at home   ☐ spend a lot of time alone

☐ take a course in anthropology   ☐ learn about culture shock

☐ talk to someone who has lived abroad   ☐ visit a doctor regularly

Beating Culture SHOCK

You have a chance to live and work overseas, to get to know another culture from the inside. It's a wonderful opportunity, but don't be surprised if you experience at least some culture shock. "When you're put into a new culture, even simple things can throw you. You become like a child again, unable to handle everyday life on your own," says one expert on culture shock.

Taking a course in anthropology or intercultural studies is one effective way to reduce the effects of culture shock. If you can, talk to an expatriate who has lived in the country for at least a few years. Someone who has been there can alert you to some of the things you'll need to learn.

Finally, prepare yourself by learning about culture shock itself. Someone living in a new culture typically goes through four stages of adjustment. Initial euphoria, or the honeymoon stage, is characterized by high expectations, a focus on similarities in the new culture, and a tendency to attach positive values to any differences that are noticed.

Culture shock, the second stage, begins very suddenly. The symptoms of culture shock include homesickness; feelings of anxiety, depression, fatigue, and inadequacy; and mild paranoia. Some people going through culture shock try to withdraw from the new culture, spending most of their free time reading novels about home, sleeping 12 hours a night, and associating only with others from their own country. Others eat and drink too much, feel irritable, and display hostility or even aggression.

A period of gradual adjustment is the third stage. Once you realize you're adjusting, life gets more hopeful. You've been watching what's been going on around you, and you're starting to learn the patterns and underlying values of the culture. It feels more natural, and you feel more self-assured.

The fourth stage, full adjustment, takes several years, and not everyone achieves it. A lot depends on people's personalities – how rigid or how easygoing they are – and how seriously they try to understand the new culture.

B Read the article again. Match the statements with the people who would say them.

	Stage 1 person	Stage 2 person	Stage 3 person	Stage 4 person
1. "I just want to sleep all the time."	☐	✓	☐	☐
2. "The customs here are different, but they are so wonderful and sophisticated!"	☐	☐	☐	☐
3. "I've lived here so many years that it feels like home to me."	☐	☐	☐	☐
4. "Everyone has been so helpful and friendly since I've arrived. The people here are so polite!"	☐	☐	☐	☐
5. "I'm starting to understand the culture and feel more self-assured here."	☐	☐	☐	☐
6. "I only spend time with people from my own country."	☐	☐	☐	☐